Dr. Whacko's Guide
to Slow-Pitch Softball

Dr. Whacko's Guide to Slow-Pitch Softball

BRUCE BROWN

COLLIER BOOKS
MACMILLAN PUBLISHING COMPANY
New York

COLLIER MACMILLAN CANADA
Toronto

MAXWELL MACMILLAN INTERNATIONAL
New York   Oxford   Singapore   Sydney

Collier Books
Macmillan Publishing Company
866 Third Avenue, New York, NY 10022

Collier Macmillan Canada, Inc.
1200 Eglinton Avenue East, Suite 200
Don Mills, Ontario M3C 3N1

Library of Congress Cataloging-in-Publication Data
Brown, Bruce.
    Dr. Whacko's guide to slow-pitch softball/Bruce Brown.—1st
Collier Books ed.
        p.   cm.
    ISBN 0-02-013096-1
    1. Slow pitch softball—United States.   I. Title.
GV863.A1B77   1991   90-42030   CIP
796.357′8—dc20

First Collier Books Edition 1991

10 9 8 7 6 5 4 3 2 1

Printed in the United States of America

For Orville Bailey,
Sidney Lambert,
the Buddha of Missoula,
and everybody on the old Spuds team—
"BE A POTATO!"

Contents

Introduction

The first thing I should probably admit is that I've always had a hard time resisting the roar of a distant crowd on a summer night.

When I was a kid, I used to ride my bike out to the ball fields on the outskirts of town after dinner. I could steer by the aureole of light above the ballpark, although I had to close my eyes when I passed through the low places where insects were particularly thick.

I'd slide into the wooden bleachers next to the concession stand in the second or third inning. Often the town patriarchs sat nearby, including Raymond Oliver, for whom the field was named. Raymond had been principal of the consolidated high school for decades, but before that he played semipro baseball, where he got the nickname that every kid in town knew but none dared call him to his face.

When "Wire Tail" Raymond and the town of Nooksack, Oregon, were growing up together, the game they played here was baseball, or what used to be called "old-fashioned country hardball." A crackerjack shortshop, Raymond began playing for money before he was out of high school. He might have pursued the game further, but after being gassed in World War I, he turned to teaching school and coaching fast-pitch softball, which was then eclipsing

INTRODUCTION

baseball as the most popular participant sport of the American countryside.

Another old-timer often on hand for evening games in the town park was Wynn Noyes, the town druggist. Wynn had pitched in the major leagues during the teens, and was on the Chicago team that allegedly threw the 1919 World Series. He made no secret of his belief that the "skinflint" Comiskeys who owned the Black Sox— and not Shoeless Joe Jackson—should have been banned from baseball. "Joe hit a *hard* .375 in the World Series, and they gave him the boot," he'd spit disgustedly.

Other times, Wynn liked to reminisce about kooky things from his own war-shortened career, like the time when a Boston Braves rookie, Les Mann, lined a double into the gap against the New York Giants. A speedster, Mann took off for third on the next pitch. He got such a good jump that the catcher, Chief Meyers, didn't even make a throw. The problem was that one of Mann's own teammates already occupied third. Fortunately, Meyers was even more startled than Mann and when he finally did make a throw hurled the ball into left field, allowing both runners to score.

I must have heard that story a hundred times over the years. Eavesdropping on Wynn, Raymond, and their cronies drinking coffee in the grandstand, I often had the impression they weren't talking about the action on the field. It seemed they were immersed in some other game, from some other time.

Usually, they didn't pay any more attention to me than the worms in the outfield grass. Once, though, I remember Raymond Oliver turned to me after watching a particularly overpowering fast-pitch hurler strike out a batter.

"He's not on the rubber when he releases the ball," he said.

"Huh?" I replied, doing my best impersonation of a grown-up.

"Look at his feet," Raymond continued. "He's got one foot on the rubber when he starts his windup—like the rules require—but by the time he actually releases the ball he's jumped two or three feet closer to the batter. If I was the other team's coach, I'd talk to the umpire. I'd ask him to make sure the pitcher was touching the rubber at the moment *when he released the ball*."

Watching the pitcher's next delivery, I realized that Raymond was right. The thing that made the burly blond hurler so hard to hit was that he had found a way to shorten the distance from the pitcher's mound to the plate. After that, I began to look for some of the more subtle aspects of situations that can determine their outcome even though most people don't know what is going on.

This quest carried me far from Nooksack, and the games children play. There were times—years, in fact—when I could have described the stupas on the road to Kailash a lot easier than I could have hit the cutoff man on a throw from right field to third base. I didn't play softball, and frankly didn't feel any deep loss.

Eventually, though, I returned to the little town on the Nooksack River, and Raymond Oliver Park. Among the changes I noticed immediately was the blinking traffic light (the town's first) that had been installed at the corner in front of the fire hall. Out at the ball field, I found they had torn down the old two-story announcer's booth directly behind home plate and replaced it with more "grandstand" seating, which brought the capacity to 250 or more.

Raymond himself had died the winter before, which was probably just as well because the game they played out at Raymond Oliver Park was not the game he knew and loved. The softball of my youth—in which the pitcher whipped the ball underhand to the batter at speeds as high as one hundred miles per hour—had entirely vanished. The game they played now was called slow-pitch because the pitcher lobbed the ball underhand to the batter like you would to a child on the front lawn.

In the space of just a few years, slow-pitch softball became *the* American sport of summer afternoons and evenings. Unlikely devotees included presidents George Bush and Jimmy Carter, actors Woody Allen and George C. Scott, singers Barbara Mandrell and Willie Nelson, columnist Mike Royko, New York real-estate operator and media magnate Mort Zuckerman, NASA astronauts Don Williams and Steve Hawley, and even former major leaguers Doug Flynn and Ted Cox.

I really never had a desire to do *anything* that Barbara Mandrell did, so I didn't exactly jump to get involved. In fact, I thought it was an abomination at first. What changed my mind was playing the game a little. Then I could see it was a lot more fun, since there was a lot more action of all sorts: more hits, more runs, more defensive chances, more pressure pitching. I also learned early on that it was not as easy a game as it looked.

It took me years to figure out the important ways that slow-pitch softball differs from baseball and fast-pitch softball. It was easy to see the contrasts in the pitching, but in time I realized that virtually every aspect of the game differs, sometimes subtly and sometimes dramatically. As I became more involved, this combination of the familiar and foreign made me feel a little uneasy, but by then I was hooked.

I was playing a couple times a week with a bunch of guys who were about my speed. A friend called us "misfits from all walks of life," and in a way she was right. We had virtually every significant community oddball on our roster at one time or another. The names came and went, just like the names of the sponsors on our shirts. Finally I got tired of it. Deciding the time had come to rise above commercialism, I named the team the Mouth Breathers.

In the early days, people just laughed at us. Always inclined to joke around, we became known primarily for antics such as the Mouth Breather cheer, a panting chant which sounded like an iron lung run amok in a mangrove swamp. We got real loose, and in the process—like Columbus sailing west to reach the east—we became real tight as a team.

This is the improbable story of the unstoppable Mouth Breathers, a summer that didn't end until a few days after Christmas on a frozen lake, and some of the slow-pitch softball tricks that landed us in the snow drifts.

Dr. Whacko's Guide to Slow-Pitch Softball

Red Shoes Don't Make It Anymore

There is nothing this old practitioner likes seeing more than a hot young baseball player come up to bat for the first time in a slow-pitch softball game—especially on the other team.

If I'm pitching, I'll do my best dork routine. Pulling my pants up too high, I begin to twitch oddly around the mouth and eyes. Sometimes I'll even drop the ball and then kick it awkwardly as I reach to pick it up.

I remember one guy who thought I was particularly hopeless. He almost salivated as he tapped the dirt off his fancy red spikes, which matched the baseball uniform pants he was wearing with a comparatively simple slow-pitch T-shirt top.

I gave him lots of time to get himself set, which he did with the deliberate delicacy that most people reserve for handling a lethal weapon. Clearly, he was expecting to clobber the ball. "Are you ready?" I asked, twisting him a little tighter.

Tony, the catcher and father-confessor figure on our team, has spoken to me about this. "You toy with them too much," he told me once when we were celebrating a particularly satisfying slow-pitch softball tournament victory. "Why draw it out?" he asked. "The guy is just a formality."

I defended my motives—a bit too strenuously, perhaps—in terms of the aesthetics of pitching, but I did not disagree with his basic point. It doesn't matter how good a player was in fast-pitch softball or baseball. He really doesn't have much of a chance the first time he faces a good slow-pitch hurler.

The reason is that the games of baseball and slow-pitch softball are too different. Despite the fact that they both are played on diamonds with bats, gloves, bases, three strikes, and four balls, baseball and slow-pitch softball diverge in several crucial respects. To play slow-pitch softball successfully, you have to adjust not only your hitting and pitching, but also your defense and underlying strategy.

Take the guy in the red shoes. Even before the first pitch, he had already made a mistake which doomed his first turn at bat. The problem was his position in the batter's box. He took a straightaway position, with one foot in front of the plate and the other behind it. In hardball this is a good place to be. Some hitters may prefer to stand closer to the pitcher at the front of the box, and others may prefer to stand farther away at the back of the box, but straightaway is always a safe choice, especially against a pitcher you have never faced before.

In slow-pitch softball, however, straightaway is a very bad place to be. The reason is the high arc of the ball after it leaves the pitcher's hand. A strike must be lofted to a height of at least six feet, and then fall in a roughly two-square-foot area behind the plate. This means that the ball passes over the plate about head-high, or way out of the normal hitting zone. The only way to hit this pitch is to attack it with an unorthodox stroke like lumberjacks use in the double-bladed axe throw.

Fortunately, the guy in the red shoes was cool. I could tell by the way he tucked up the sleeve of his shirt like the San Francisco Giants' Will Clark that he had studied the classical forms. He would not take an ungainly hack if he could help it. And so I threw a simple strike, right down the middle of the plate. He thought it was high, stared at the umpire for a moment, and then walked away. Now he was really determined to cream the big white ball. I obliged him with a lower-arc pitch that seems impossibly fat to a hardball hitter. The ball curved from left to right, though, and it was so soft that it actually fell well in front of the plate. The umpire was just beginning to call it flat when the eager hitter swung and fouled the ball weakly off the end of the bat.

The count was now no balls and two strikes. I knew if I struck him out my team would all throw themselves to the grass as if moved by an invisible wind. This is one of the little jokes we have developed over our years of playing together. Teams that know us will sometimes even strike out on purpose just to see Dr. Whacko and the Mouth Breathers throw themselves on their backs. One cold, wet day a few years ago, an archrival tavern team struck out three times (and ended up losing the game) for the pleasure of seeing us in the mud. Today, though, the field was dry. I wanted the strikeout, so I reached deep into my bag of tricks.

I decided to try a pitch I had been working on during the week on my mound at home. It used backspin to gyroscopically curve like a screwball. When it worked it could break as much as four inches, but it didn't always break. Then it was an easy mark, like a chicken on a busy roadway. I tried to throw it as a backdoor strike—that is, a ball that starts outside but comes back at the last instant to catch the far corner of the plate. The ball broke well, but I had been too cautious, and did not come back enough. The batter watched the ball all the way down to the ground, and then stared back at the umpire as if daring him to call it a strike. Ball one.

Tony, who was catching as usual, got up out of his crouch behind the plate and threw the ball back with authority that spoke in the crack of the ball in my glove. I came back with high arc, which is both the statistically hardest to throw for a strike, and the hardest to hit if it drops in. Because the ball can come down from a height of twelve feet (or more in some leagues), a high-arc pitch must be intercepted in that brief moment when it falls through the plane of the batter's swing. This is much harder than you'd think. It's also much different from baseball or fast-pitch softball, where the bat and pitched ball occupy the same plane much longer. But my high-arc pitch was deep, falling too far behind the plate.

The count was now two balls and two strikes, and I could hear Tony's words in my mind. Now I had to throw a strike, and the guy in red shoes knew it. I thought, well, he hasn't had a good swing yet. Let's see him hit it. So I threw the same pitch I started with, simple backspin right down the middle of the plate. He still hadn't adjusted his position in the batter's box, and so once again the pitch seemed high to him. He knew he had to swing at anything close, though, so he took a rip. It was the best swing he'd had yet, but because of the height of the pitch, he was forced to uppercut the ball, lofting it deep into right-center field.

I turned and watched Boo, our right-center fielder, drifting back under the tall lights, calling and waving his arms. The ball was in his sights, and since we were playing on a field without fences, there was nothing to stop him from going and getting it. He drifted back another half dozen or so strides, and then gathered it in his grasp, which was as soft and icy as a foot of new-fallen snow.

Back on the bench, Tony caught my eye. I knew what he was going to say so I answered him before he could ask. "Just working on my reputation as a mental case," I said.

DR. WHACKO'S NOTEBOOK

No. 1: Basic Positioning in the Batter's Box

1. As you step up to the plate to hit, think where you are going to stand because a poor choice can take you out before the first pitch.

2. To maximize your chances, you've got to be able to hit the strikes. If you can't, a decent slow-pitch hurler will play with you in public.

3. During practice, go up to the plate and position yourself where you need to be to take the ball that falls just behind the plate for a quality strike. Insist on strikes during batting practice so that you get in the habit of recognizing and swinging at good pitches.

4. Most hitters playing in rec leagues should be standing deeper in the box than they would in baseball.

2

Revenge of
the Mouth Breathers

All losses aren't the same, no matter what the won-lost column says. There are times—and ways—to blow games that are especially awful. Sometimes, it is possible to lose a game so horribly that even the winning team feels embarrassed by the outcome, as if it has been cheapened by just being on the same field with the loser.

In the early days, Dr. Whacko and the Mouth Breathers specialized in this kind of finale. Despite the fact that most of us were at least modestly good players, we got to the point where we almost dreaded taking a lead into the late innings. It was less traumatic to get the business of losing over early in the game.

I remember one time we were nervously protecting a one-run lead in the top of the seventh inning. We got two outs, while the other team loaded the bases—putting the tying and winning runners into scoring position on third and second base. Their next batter scorched a line drive right at our second baseman, Zoomie. He raised his glove to take the ball, but somehow it glanced off the tip.

He still had time to get the out if he could retrieve the ball and get the runner coming down the line from first.

Zoomie spun around like an enraged Chihuahua and scampered after the ball to the edge of the outfield grass. He got to it quickly enough, and might have still gotten the runner at second if he flipped it to our shortstop covering the bag. Zoomie was determined to eliminate any more chances for error, though, so he decided to make the putout himself.

Unfortunately, he stumbled as he started for second base, only a few feet away. Sprawling on his knees, he tried to do a sort of crab-crawl to the bag. Meantime the runner was flying down the line and going into his slide. In desperation, Zoomie lunged full length and slithered "on his belly like a rep-tile." The runner was safe and all Zoomie got was a face full of dirt. Needless to say, the next batter singled, and we lost the game.

Another time, we had a sure out in the last inning, but the ball eluded our first baseman, Freeman. He grabbed it on the rebound off the fence post, though, and threw to second base. The throw beat the runner to the bag, but unfortunately it hit him in the back, allowing him to scamper over to third base, where he slowed down long enough to notice that our catcher, Tony, was out of position near the mound. This meant no one was covering home plate. So the runner trotted home with the winning run on what should have been the third out, and we couldn't do anything but watch.

It wasn't too long after this that we once again found ourselves in the nerve-wracking position of leading going into the last inning of a Sunday afternoon game. Almost immediately, the game took an ominous turn. The first batter on the other team doubled into the gap, and then scored on another ringing drive to left. Quicker than you could say "humiliation," the other team had loaded the bases, putting the potential winning run on third with no one out. Things looked pretty bleak for the Mouth Breathers from where I stood in the outfield.

Boo, our right-center fielder, and I were having a typically meaningless outfield conversation in which I understood maybe one word in four. I said I hoped his dad had a good stand of hay on his place. Boo looked at me like I was crazy. "Hey, don't *you* be standing," he called back. The youngest player on our team, Boo was always in motion, and just as rarely in uniform. He didn't like to wear a hat because it crushed his carefully cultivated hairstyle, which Tony once dubbed "Night of the Living Mohawk."

At six foot two—not counting the mohawk—Boo was an impressive sight, and something of a local legend. Even in street clothes, it was obvious that he had an exceptionally strong upper body. Boo had been a state champion wrestler in high school. He was still notorious locally for the time he and his father were loading hogs to take to the butcher. One got away, and they had to grab it and carry it to the truck. When Boo released his neck-lock on the animal it didn't move. He had strangled it.

That was the summer he was seventeen. He was twenty-three when he began playing for the lowly Mouth Breathers, but already he had a lot more outfield experience than anyone else on the team. I used to marvel at the smoothness and poise of his play. He was fast enough to outrun a lot of line drives, and he had the best arm I ever saw in slow-pitch softball. One time I asked him how he threw so hard. He said part of the trick was getting your feet set.

"It isn't like the infield out here, you know," he said. "The important thing isn't to get rid of the ball quickly.

The important thing is to make your throw strong and accurate—and you can't do that if you don't have your feet planted." I looked down at his feet, which were shod in laceless search-and-rescue green water booties with octopus-like suction cups on the bottom, instead of baseball spikes.

"I think my feet are just fine," I replied. "It's my arm that I'm worried about."

"You got something wrong with your arm?" Boo asked in his bored-seeming kind of way.

I admitted that I had blown my arm out as a teenager when I threw too many curves pitching hardball. "Well, I know one thing you might try. I learned it from an uncle who played outfield in the Cardinals' farm system."

Boo had me take a ball in my right (throwing) hand, and raise it to shoulder level straight in front of me, with my palm on top of the ball. "Make like you're throwing the ball," he said. When I had finished, he had me raise the ball in front of me again. "Now roll your hand a little counterclockwise, and make like you're throwing the ball."

The moment I tried it, I could see the difference. When I rotated my hand counterclockwise just a little, I was forced to draw the ball back behind my ear in the classic throwing position. I also noticed that my arm had more snap, like a rubber band under tension, when it came around. It was a delicate adjustment, like everything associated with the arm and throwing. Cranking the throwing hand over too much not only hurt the throw, it hurt the arm and opened the way to injury. Just a little twist made a big difference, though. It also made me approach the outfield differently knowing that I had at least a couple of good throws in my arm.

Now, in the bottom of the seventh, it looked like we were about to lose another game. What were the odds that we could get three outs before they snuck at least one run across the plate? I personally would not have bet on it. Still, Boo and I crept in several steps so that we could have a chance to get the runner at the plate on a fly ball. "If I can get to it, let me make the throw," Boo said as the pitch arced toward the plate. Before I could answer "OK," the batter stroked the ball on a sinking line to center. Normally I would have tried for the ball, but this time I let Boo get it.

Cutting behind to back him up if necessary, I had a great view as he scooped the ball off his shoe tops for the first out. With his momentum still carrying him toward the plate, he came up throwing in one smooth motion like a classical javelin thrower. The runner on third had broken for home when he gloved the ball, and he was most of the way there when Boo's throw hissed past the head of the cutoff man, Zoomie, heading directly to the plate. Sweet and unexpected as wild strawberries in the weeds, Boo's throw bounced twice to Tony, who swept his mitt down to cleanly and clearly tag the runner out for a double play.

That was the first time I ever embraced anyone with a twenty-two-inch neck and moussed mohawk. I couldn't believe his throw. We were in a position where we had to execute perfectly to avoid getting beat, and we had done it. Most of us on the field were, I think, frankly astounded. We felt strange and unaccustomed to our outward appearance, like caterpillars who had suddenly become butterflies.

We weren't out of trouble yet, of course. There were still two outs and runners on first and second. It was a funny thing, though. Now we all knew that the other team wasn't going to get the runner home. We *knew* that each of us was going to do whatever it took to win the game.

The pop fly to our shortstop, Rod, which ended the game and gave us the win, was almost an anti-climax. The most important play of the game—and, in fact, that entire season—was Boo's throw to the plate.

After that, we simply did not lose very often. The full effects weren't obvious until the next season, but that throw began the Mouth Breathers' revenge.

DR. WHACKO'S NOTEBOOK

No. 2: The Importance of Defense

1. Good defense pumps up a team *as a whole* more than good hitting. All it takes is one superlative—or even good—play to turn a team around and show it what it's capable of.

2. Although most players concentrate on offensive aspects of the game, good glove-work decides at least as many contests as hitting. It's hard to make such comparisons, but a great catch and throw can be worth as much as a home run.

3. In the outfield, take the time necessary to set your feet, and visually pick up your cutoff man, before making the throw. It is more important to make a strong, accurate throw than it is to get rid of the ball the instant it touches your hands.

4. It is possible to increase the snap on long throws from the outfield by twisting your hand *just a little* counterclockwise (for right-handed throwers) as you draw the ball back. This forces the person throwing the ball to draw it behind the ear in the classic position, and puts perhaps 15 percent more zip in the throw.

3

Patented Weenie Elixir

Some people call him lucky, but I have played with him long enough to know that what he has is not luck.

For one thing, luck is not something you can control. Luck does not let you dunk game-winning hits into left field four games in a row, any more than it can give you an unbroken string of statuesque girlfriends.

What Zoomie has can do this, though. I've seen it for years, ever since we met playing pickup ball one evening in Raymond Oliver Park. We felt a natural affinity that began with sharing the cheapest brand of drinkable beer, and quickly extended to more esoteric subjects like how to combat mushroom growth in the back seat of a '62 Plymouth.

Before the end of the summer, I had become quite fond of Zoomie—we called him Ned then—and his first wife, Sheila. She was one of the most striking women I had ever seen, with river-blue eyes and golden hair down to the middle of her back. She also had a sweet sense of humor. Once after I had forgotten my hat at their place, she safety-pinned it to my coat.

By comparison, Zoomie did not make too much of a first impression. He was about average height or a little under, with a shock of black hair and dark shiny eyes. His premature paunch made him look like he was last in line for everything but meals, and he had a gift for the gauche. He once told me without any trace of embarrassment that he threw up in Sheila's shoes on their first date.

And yet, Zoomie was a great romantic figure to many who knew him. A dreamer at heart, he lived for the figments of his imagination, not his amazingly dysfunctional house, old car, or mundane job. He always had something going, and his schemes were generally as funky as they were grand. More than anybody else I ever knew, he had an ability to triumph through what others took to be mistakes.

In the chronicle of Zoomie's graver errors, his family counted the decision to go to technical school rather than college especially heinous. Even though his father was a department chairman at the University of Washington in Seattle, Zoomie decided he wanted to be a nurse. A lot of people thought Zoomie was closing the door on his own future, but actually he was positioning himself for much more ambitious adventures than academe could provide.

Sharp and irrepressibly enthusiastic, he proved to be an excellent nurse. Before long he was supervising an entire ward at a big Seattle hospital. His family were just beginning to accommodate themselves to his "career decision" (as his father invariably called it) when Zoomie quit. Learning that owners of large, ocean-going yachts sometimes hire people to ferry their boats across the Atlantic or Pacific, he talked Sheila and himself onto a seventy-two-foot ketch headed for Sydney, Australia. Eighteen months later he returned, but Sheila did not.

His family expected him to get another job at a big hospital, but he surprised them again. He landed a job at the public health clinic in Crescent City, seven miles west of Nooksack. There he met Margaret, who ran the cross-country skiing shop on the North Fork Road. They climbed high rock faces, and hung together in bivouac sacks like bats. After her came Ellen, an astronomer at the state observatory who gave him his nickname. "Zoomie" was supposedly what he said when she first showed him the rings of Saturn through a twenty-power telescope.

Zoomie and I played slow-pitch softball together almost every summer during those years (another mistake in the eyes of his family). He was a good fielder, but the thing he did best was hit. From the beginning he had a marvelous sense of slow-pitch hitting tactics. He became a truly feared hitter not by slugging the ball harder or farther than anyone else—in fact, there were several people on our team who surpassed him on both counts. What Zoomie did better than anyone else was to shake singles out of the mixed bag of grounders and humpbacked liners that everybody hits.

He realized that the main difference between slow-pitch and hardball is not the high-arc pitch (Rip Sewell had his "eephus" pitch, which Ted Williams hit for a home run in the 1946 All-Star Game), or the aluminum bats (which are today used at all levels of softball and hardball, except the American professional leagues). The main difference is the extra fielder that most teams employ as a fourth outfielder. With this sort of defensive alignment, a ball hit to the infield has just about the same chance of going through for a base hit as it does in hardball. A ball lofted into the outfield, however, has a statistically greater chance of being caught.

To hit for high average in slow-pitch softball, it is necessary to spread the fielders as much as possible. To do this, the best batters hit to more than one field. Zoomie's hitting, for instance, follows a pattern as much as the pitchers' offerings to the plate. While the better pitchers are working him in and out, he is working the other team's defense, spreading it out like soft dough on a stick. Each at-bat sets up what follows, so that he actually becomes more dangerous late in a game when the opposition has already seen him hit a couple times.

The year the Mouth Breathers became a championship club, Zoomie was brilliant. I remember one game early that summer when he almost single-handedly destroyed the other team. Coming up to bat the first time, he typically looked for a pitch he could pull down the third base line. Opposite-field hitting is probably his greatest strength, but the game was young and he did not want to try that until he had tested the other team. Even if he hit a limp grounder, he would force the third baseman or shortstop to make a long throw, which he might be able to beat out for a hit. And if the infielders weren't awake, a sharply hit grounder might dart through untouched.

This time the third baseman was wide awake, back-handing Zoomie's one-hopper deep behind the bag. His momentum carried him into foul territory, where he wheeled and slung a seed to the first baseman, getting Zoomie by a stride. A lot of players come back to the bench in a bad mood after making an out like that, but Zoomie seemed typically unperturbed. To him, an out is as good as a hit for setting up his next at-bat. Either way, the other team now thought of him as a pull hitter. And in the meantime, he provided a bit of vital intelligence for the rest of our lineup, which now began probing for weaknesses at positions other than third.

When Zoomie came up the next time, the other team's infield shifted deeper into the hole to handle a ball that had been pulled. In the outfield, the left and left-center fielders came up on their toes, the right-center fielder watched with interest, and the right fielder was suddenly struck with the solution to his car's transmission problem. With a runner on first, the defense would normally encourage the hitter to pull the ball in hope of a double play, but because the pitcher thought Zoomie *wanted* to pull it, he threw him pitches which were hard to pull—and ideal for hitting to right. Zoomie hit one slicing down the right-field line past the now fully engaged right fielder, giving him a triple and scoring the runner all the way from first base.

That stroke is one of Zoomie's favorites, and one of his most powerful. It is worth noting, however, that the ball did not travel as far as the right fielder in the air. The same line drive to left would probably have been a single. Hit to right off the bat of a right-handed hitter, however, the ball had a slicing spin which carried it away from the pursuing fielder. Once it skipped past, the fielder was forced to chase it while Zoomie rounded the bases. The only question was whether it would be a homer. The right fielder had to really dig and peg to hold Zoomie to a standup triple.

Just like the groundout before it, Zoomie's triple also helped set up his next turn at bat. There are few sights that stick in outfielders' minds more than the back of one of their brethren as he pursues a ball that has gotten through. Late in the game, when the outfielders are especially loath to let a hit get by for extra bases, this means two or three steps. Good outfielders will lay back that much out of grudging respect for a batter on the other team who has burned them. Zoomie often commands this respect, although he seldom actually hits the ball over the outfielders' heads.

The game came to its climax in the bottom of the fifth. The Mouth Breathers had risen up to score five runs in the inning and take a 12–3 lead. If we scored one more run, the umpire would terminate the game and declare us winner by virtue of a ten-run advantage. There were runners at first and third and one out when Zoomie stepped up to the plate. The infield was creeping in, hoping for the double play that would get them out of the inning. The outfield, meanwhile, was gathered close to each foul line and as deep as they dared with a runner at third.

Knowing that a hit of any kind or even a decent fly ball would win the game, Zoomie planned to hit the ball up the middle. He swung at the first pitch, but the ball broke in on him so that he hit it weakly off the handle— rather than the head—of the bat. The shortstop turned and scrambled back just as the left-center fielder began sprinting in. Ordinarily the ball would have been a fairly routine play for the shortstop, but because the infield was drawn in, and because they played him to hit down the lines, the ball fell just beyond his leaping dive.

Too much! Even though our opponent's defense had been intelligently positioned, and the pitcher had enticed the batter to swing at a bad pitch which effectively nullified his power, we had won. For Zoomie's ball to fall seemed like a cruel twist of fate to the players on the other team, but there was actually a simple explanation.

Most good hitters know they have to move the ball around to be successful, but Zoomie is one of the few I've met who understands that he can move the fielders, too. This realization gives him a substantial tactical advantage. It's as if he has a whole other set of knobs to twist in the ever-changing game of adjustment and counteradjustment.

For that game, Zoomie had two hits in three at-bats, two RBI, the game-winning RBI, and a slugging percentage over 1.000. Yet he only hit the ball well once, and even then his triple didn't fly as far as Rod's double.

"Who is this Zoo Meat?" Boo called loudly, repeating an ancient, sanctified insult that came from a similar victim of Zoomie's long ago.

"Hey, I thought that shortstop was gonna start bawling at the end there," said Marlon, our slight right fielder. He giggled as he opened a cooler full of tall-necked bottles of imported beer on ice.

Everyone took a bottle except Zoomie, who begged off on account of a previous engagement. He quickly changed his spikes and slid behind the wheel of his old Volvo.

"Gotta boogie," he said. "I got a date."

"Her name is Cynthia," Tony observed as the Volvo sprung to life.

Then Zoomie was gone, leaving the married to argue with the hitless about the nature of luck.

DR. WHACKO'S NOTEBOOK

No. 3: Basic Hitting Tactics

1. Forget the underhanded pitching and metal bats. The biggest single difference between slow-pitch softball and baseball is the extra outfielder. The tenth man tips the averages in favor of the defense, and makes it statistically more likely that fly balls to the outfield will be caught.

2. It's possible to hit for a high average in slow-pitch (in fact, the best hitters routinely hit over .500), but to achieve this kind of success you've got to make adjustments in both the physical and mental aspects of hitting.

3. Once you've ironed out the kinks in your batting stroke, think about the pattern of your hitting through a game. Each turn at bat should set up your following turns at the plate by exposing weaknesses in the defense's personnel or alignment. Remember, you can move the fielders around as much as you move the ball around.

4. You don't have to hit to "all" fields to spread the fielders. Two fields can be enough to give you a temporary advantage. That's why almost any weenie can be a feared hitter in slow-pitch softball.

4

The Best Are Boring

Next to a sunny day and a new ball, the thing that softball players probably like best is a good story. Everybody's got one, and there are times when it's impossible to stop them from being told.

You hear them among teammates at victory celebrations, with spouses at home after the game, among strangers the next day in the elevator, and finally on your patio years later while the children are in the basement setting the dog on fire.

Most share a heavy-handed heroism, but there are also some significant differences, especially between the stories of hitters and pitchers. Even when they're describing the same incident, hitters' and pitchers' stories can sound like they came from opposite coasts.

For instance, a guy I know likes to tell the story of a game in which he faced Dr. Whacko and the Mouth Breathers. He waxes poetic describing how the west wind was blowing straight in from center field that afternoon, pasting leaves and candy wrappers to the chain-link backstop, and making it impossible for anyone to wear a hat.

I had shut out Bud's team to that point, but we had scored only three runs ourselves. There were two runners on base, and his teammates were jumping up and down on their bench, hollering. Because of the wind, which was gusting twenty-five miles per hour, we drew our outfield in, hoping to cut the run off at the plate.

Wind is usually an ally of the good slow-pitch hurler because moving air makes it possible to curve the ball more, but it doesn't always work that way. The first pitch I threw Bud hung in the air like a sobbing "good-bye," and then descended meekly to meet the bright bat that smashed it on a clean line toward left-center field. The first thing I heard after the crack of the bat was our shortstop Rod's urgent, one-word command to the out-field: "Back!"

It was already too late, though. Even then the ball was sailing a dozen feet over our left-center fielder's head as it bored straight into the teeth of the gale. Bud trotted across home plate about the time the distant fielder was retrieving the ball. At that point, Zoomie came to the mound and asked me, "You got any more of those up your sleeve?" Peering up my jersey, I replied, "I don't think more than one would fit." In thirty years of watching softball, I have never seen a ball hit harder.

I like to tell Bud's story, too, but in the pitcher's eyes, it takes a different shape. I don't end it with him crossing the plate to the jubilation of his teammates. I go on to mention that after we got the third out, I passed Bud on the way to the bench. "Nice hit," I said, adding in a friendly, matter-of-fact tone, "you'll never see that pitch again." And it was true. Knowing he could punish a pitch up and out over the plate, I decided to try the pitch that is probably a weakness of more hitters than any other, namely the inside strike.

After his big three-run homer into the gale (actually, small-craft warnings were posted), I never gave Bud anything on the outside part of the plate. I got Bud to pop out to Zoomie his last time up, and the Mouth Breathers went on to win the windy game, 5–3. Bud and I played against each other for a couple more years, but he never got another extra-base hit off me. I'm not sure he ever realized what happened, though. Like so many, he just thought he was overdue for another big hit off the ever-wily Dr. Whacko.

Why don't hitters like Bud adjust? I believe the reason is that pitchers' stories are so boring nobody pays much attention. Listening to a pitcher talk is like observing a slow, inevitable process, like the erosion of a mountain or a middle-aged person gaining weight. In fact, to succeed at pitching in slow-pitch softball, you must approach your task like the chefs who prepare the dessert tables at fancy hotels. Your job is to present your wares to the hitter in the most attractive manner possible, even though they generally are not good for him. Since you cannot prevent the batter from hitting the ball, you want to tempt him to indulge his weaknesses.

Sometimes you can tell by looking at the hitter's feet what kind of pitch will give him trouble (if he's even with the plate, he may not be able to hit a high strike; if he's a "normal" distance from the plate, he may not be able to hit an inside strike, etc.). Other times, you need to see a hitter swing to understand his appetite and ability. Good hitters are good hitters, but at the recreational level, most batters have at least one area of relative weakness. To be successful, the slow-pitch pitcher needs to live in that narrow zone where the odds are the least hostile.

Compared to swaggering fast-pitch softball hurlers, their slow-pitch counterparts are an unassuming lot. The pitcher remains the single most important player on the field, though. And it may not happen often, but slow-pitch pitchers can still dominate the game.

That certainly was true the Mouth Breathers' big season, when one of our relief pitchers threw the only no-hitter I've ever seen in slow-pitch softball. It was a balmy evening in mid-July, and the Mouth Breathers were playing a team from the neighboring town who could fairly be characterized as free swingers. We had already beaten them once that season in a game that was close until the sixth, when we broke it open. They had some good players, but they were all young and tended to be streaky.

Our pitcher that night at Raymond Oliver Park was Freeman, the president of Valley Trust & Savings Bank. That sounded impressive, but actually Freeman's title was bigger than the bank, which had one branch at the back of the River View Shopping Center. He usually didn't pitch—first base was his normal position—but for some reason I had decided to shake up the lineup.

That night on the mound, Freeman seemed preoccupied. He had to drive to Prineville on business the next day, and I guessed he was eager to get home and pack. Everybody else was in an ebullient mood, though, especially after we jumped out to a quick lead. The full moon was rising out of the volcanic summit of Three Fingered Jack when we came up to bat in the fifth inning. As if on cue, we scored four runs to ten-run the opposition and abruptly conclude the game.

The win was a particularly sweet one for us because it gave us exclusive possession of first place. When we got off to a quick start that year, people said we would fade. At the halfway mark in the season, though, we were still in first place. It was all a little too much to believe, and so we were already a little giddy when Freeman said, "You know, I don't think any of those guys got a hit off me."

"You're kidding," I said, grabbing the scorebook and studying the record of the game. Freeman had walked two batters (actually the same batter twice), and Rod had made a rare error at shortstop, but those were the only base runners. The other team didn't have a hit. Freeman, who some people call "Small Change," had accomplished one of the rarest of pitching triumphs, throwing a slow-pitch no-hitter.

Needless to say, Freeman loved to tell the story of this game, but it became a kind of curse. He couldn't stop talking about it, and the more he talked about it the less people wanted to hear. "Remember how that big muscular guy—the left fielder—grounded out *three times in a row?*" he'd ask expectantly.

"Pretty amazing," Rod finally said in his deadpan Indian way. Freeman got a little hot, but I told him to forget it.

"They're hitters," I said. "It's better they don't understand some things."

DR. WHACKO'S NOTEBOOK
No. 4: Basic Pitching Tactics

1. The basic task of the slow-pitch hurler *isn't* to prevent the batter from hitting the ball. It's to make him hit it to a fielder.

2. The trick is to make the batter swing at a pitch that he likes, but which is not really good for him.

3. Throwing strikes is the essential first step toward mastering the average slow-pitch hitter. You'd be surprised how many batters can't hit a strike (see Notebook No. 1 above, and No. 5 below).

4. Don't be offended if no one notices when you pitch a great game. The best pitchers are so boring that few hitters pay enough attention to adjust.

5

A Few Minutes
With U Jane

"Is that how men do it?" the tall woman with the gray eyes asked as she took the ball from me.

I had just spent ten minutes talking about pitching, pointing out as briskly as possible a few tricks to help recreational-league hurlers throw strikes. I talked about always striding the same, and otherwise keeping the delivery to the plate consistent.

Going through the basic parts of the pitcher's motion, I stressed the importance of being able to isolate each element, and understand how it affects the pitch. The reason, I said, is that *every* pitcher has streaks of wildness. The thing that distinguishes winners from losers is the ability to adjust; to see what's going wrong, and know what has to be done to correct it.

To illustrate my point, I stepped up on the rubber and proceeded to throw a couple of pitches which fell way outside to a right-handed batter. Turning back to the two dozen or so pitchers standing in a semicircle behind me, I said, "OK, the count is two balls and no strikes. I need to throw a strike. What do I do now?" After a respectful moment of silence, I told them an embarrassing story.

Early in my career as a slow-pitch hurler, I walked a batter on a couple of close pitches. The next batter walked a little quicker, and by the third batter I was in an absolute sweat. The strike zone seemed to have shrunk to the size of a contact lens, and my pitches were falling more and more wildly to the outside. I walked the bases full, and then walked the next batter (the fourth in a row) on four straight pitches to force in a run. Moments later I was heading off the field with my head hung down.

Before I got to the dugout, I heard the umpire say to our catcher, "All the pitches were coming off his thumb." Instantly, I knew he was right. I had noticed in practice before the game that if my thumb was the last thing that touched the ball, it would fly uncontrollably outside. Under the pressure of the game situation, however, I forgot. So when things started going bad, I didn't know how to do anything but *hope* the next pitch would be a strike. Next time, I promised myself, I was going to do something before it was too late. "The problem is in your hand," I told the assembled pitchers, "but the solution is in your head."

Now Jane Hastings, my coinstructor at the parks department seminar, took her turn on the mound. I had played with her—and against her—for years in coed slow-pitch leagues, where she was known pretty universally by the name U Jane. She started off by stepping to the rubber and gathering her hands together in front of her, seemingly meditating on a tree behind the backstop. Then she threw a beautiful high-arc strike that nipped the black on the plate and scooted away to the left like a marmot that had just sighted a hawk.

After lofting a couple more strikes with equal ease, she turned and said, "I really don't have many rules or regulations for pitching. For me it is more a feeling—an internal attitude that I try to embody. I consciously try to ignore all the distractions of the game." It was true that U Jane had unusual powers of concentration, for I have seen her on the mound while her youngest daughter was crying on the sidelines, and she didn't even twitch.

If you spend time at softball diamonds around here, sooner or later you are bound to hear some kind of strange things about U Jane. And not just your garden-variety strange, either. I've been told she worships a green flame inside her that is the spirit of a seven-thousand-year-old saber-toothed tiger. I've also heard that the oddly shaped amber she wears on a thong around her neck is an oriental fetish. I personally don't put much stock in these kinds of stories, but it is true that she believes in some things that most people around here don't know how to pronounce.

I remember an evening several winters ago when we were playing volleyball at the local high-school gym. Rod jammed his middle finger blocking a spike. Crumpling to the floor, he grabbed his hand and howled with pain. Jane went to him immediately and made him show her the injured hand. Taking it in her hands, she sort of cocked her head. Then a small but astounding thing happened. The swelling in the finger diminished visibly, like a balloon losing air. After about a minute, Rod took his hand back, and flexed it. "Wow," he said. "There's no pain. How did you do that?"

Jane studied him for an instant, like an extraterrestrial in a late-night movie trying to decide how much truth the human could handle. With most people she would have laughed the question off, but the fact that Rod was an Indian made her say more than she otherwise would have. Rod really wasn't a very traditional Indian, but as a kid he had spent some time with an uncle on Vancouver Island who was well known as a medicine man. "It's called *Reiki*," Jane told Rod matter-of-factly. "It's a form of spiritual healing. I channeled the healing energy from my hands into your injured finger. You may notice a little stiffness, but by tomorrow your finger will feel like nothing happened."

Janie smiled disarmingly at the pitchers assembled around the mound, much as she had when she got through with Rod's finger. Although she did not say anything about pain paths or violet-green flames, she did present a different approach to slow-pitch softball pitching. If I had spoken for the head, she spoke for the heart; if I had spoken for calculated competition, she spoke for the power of personal peace. She said she never wanted to "get" or "hurt" the other team. Her goal, she said, wasn't to be better than someone else. She was just trying to be the best she herself could be.

I remember how Janie's attitudes about competition used to drive me crazy when we played on the same team. You could just about count on her getting a weirdly beatific look in her eyes at the crucial point in the game. While the infield tensed up on their toes, she tranced-out. I used to think she made slow-pitch softball an isometric exercise in personal spirituality. In fact, my view of her went through a general period of darkness that was not helped by the fact that she was outpitching me by a considerable degree. At first I disparaged her rise as the team's number-one starter, but watching her week after week that summer, I came to appreciate her exceptional steadiness and grace.

I saw her throw works of art which fell right on the corner, punctuating the umpire's strike call with mute but undeniable marks in the dust. I also saw the nice things she did—such as bringing food from the concession stands—for the others on the team. Janie even got juice for Carla, our sometime third baseman, when she knew Carla was having an affair with her long-time housemate, John the abstract expressionist. The sight of Janie with her arm around Carla on the bench used to amaze me. But in the end I just took it as another example of her refusal to compete in a way that was intended to hurt others.

On the mound, U Jane presented a memorable picture with her dark wavy hair and riot of freckles splashed all over her strong thighs and shoulders. Although the color and style of the uniforms she wore over the years changed, she never wore a hat. Her windup was simple and direct, but she still could be a tremendously deceptive pitcher. Her secret was the break she got on the ball. I know that some noted slow-pitch coaches, like Oregon's George Perry, say "there is no way any amount of spin can affect a slow pitch." All I can say is they never saw U Jane, for she got great movement on the ball, and spin was her game.

I thought of her as a classic side-spin pitcher, which is to say she rolled the ball as she released it so that the ball corkscrewed along its path to the plate. She did not put a huge amount of spin on the ball, but the spin it had carried it along a complex arc. Her pitches often had two distinct trajectories, the first part up to the apogee, and then the latter part down to the ground. To hit her, the batter had to adjust to the fact that the angle and motion of the ball changed perceptibly during flight.

Depending on the angle, the wind, and the spin, her pitches could break wildly, yet she always seemed to have finger-tip control.

She explained it all differently, of course. "The most important part of the pitch isn't something that happens way over there on the other side of the plate. It isn't separated from you by forty-three feet. The most important part of the pitch begins as soon as you release the ball from your hand. It is the flight of the ball in the air, and you're directly connected to it." U Jane paused to let this sink in, and then continued. "Another thing. I never try to sight in on the catcher's mitt. I really don't pay any attention to a target like that. In fact, I never watch to see where the ball falls. What I watch is its spin in flight. I know that if the pitch is right then, it will be right when it gets to the plate."

At that point, she called for a volunteer from the audience. Choosing a man in his thirties, she ushered him to the rubber and instructed him to concentrate on the arc of the ball in the air, not its destination. She also told him to aim at a tree standing in the distance, not at the plate. He wound up and threw a perfect strike. Jane tried to stop her talk then, saying she wanted to quit while she was ahead, but the crowd wouldn't let her. They surrounded her for a quarter hour afterward to ask questions one-on-one.

I stayed and listened, too. U Jane and I had a long and complex relationship. We blew cold and hot, and I guess it's no secret there was a time when I loved her wildly. I remember sitting on the bench watching her pitch in shorts and a T-shirt one afternoon when one of the other women on our team leaned over and said to me, "You ought to go home and put ice cubes on your eyes the way welders do."

Actually, we were never more than good friends. Maybe that's why I kept hanging around making a fool of myself. When I originally heard we were going to be on the pitching seminar together, I volunteered to drive U Jane back to her place afterward.

We were cruising down the River Road chatting about a couple of mutual friends who had gotten married when a sand-colored dove flew up even with the car. Almost as soon as we saw it, the bird dropped out of sight beneath the river bank.

Then it returned to fly alongside the car again, before dipping down below the bank like before. We both watched the bird, and when it did not appear the third time, U Jane said to me, "Someone is going to die."

DR. WHACKO'S NOTEBOOK

No. 5: Control Pitching

1. The first step toward control as a pitcher is standardizing your motion. Find a type of pitch and windup that is comfortable and seems to work, and stick with it until you know it inside out.

2. Every pitcher has streaks of wildness, but there is something you can do about it if you know your own tendencies, or weaknesses.

3. Become familiar with the basic parts of your delivery (stride, release, jump back, etc.) and how each affects your pitching so you can quickly diagnose the problem when things don't go quite right.

4. If you have trouble zeroing in on the strike zone, try using a tree or some other object behind the plate in the distance as your target. You may find that focusing on a target high above the plate also makes it easier to throw high-arc pitches.

6

Dr. Whacko, I Presume

I get asked about my nickname a fair amount—where did it come from, what does it mean, can I perform gynecological examinations?

I know how the name originated, but in all honesty, I'm less sure what it means today than I was ten years ago. That was when I hit a game-winning grand-slam homer, and a teammate greeted me at the plate with a grinning, "Dr. Whacko, I presume."

I'll admit I liked it, but once the name stuck, it seemed to take on a life of its own. As I became known for switch pitching and installing a batting machine in my backyard, guys began tapping their heads with their forefingers when they said it.

Then the computer statistics sealed the "mental" image for many people. When I showed up at practice with a thick sheaf of stats, my own teammates looked at me with a horrible fascination, as if they were watching a house burn down.

Baseball has had a long bittersweet love affair with statistics, of course, as have so many of its devotees. I don't think I'm the only schoolboy who finally learned long division so I could figure out my own batting average. For nearly a century, this familiar three-digit representation of batting prowess has probably been the most immediately recognizable percentage in our culture.

Although the lust for stats clearly predates the computer, there is no denying that computerization has fueled the frenzy for figures, while simultaneously raising the level of statistical accuracy and analysis. Along the way, computer paper with perforated rip-and-tear margins has become as much a part of the baseball scene as the batting glove: although inessential, it has nonetheless become almost *de rigueur*.

The richest private trove of American softball statistics I know personally belongs to Missoula's Ken Shugart. The manager of a storied Northside squad called Red Pies Over Montana, Shugart has kept records for a decade detailing the performance of everyone on the Pies, and everyone they have played. He is able to look back and see the entire history of his team, from the footnotes to the grand triumphs, all in the merciless perspective of the percentages.

Shugart uses a program he wrote for his Commodore 64 to keep track of his stats. He started with that setup, and he has never changed, even though it has become laughably cramped for his needs. Others, like the Buddha of Missoula, use commercial programs. The Enlightened One keeps stats on an IBM AT–compatible machine with The Baseball Statbook. He has all the power and speed that Shugart lacks, but in terms of amenities his program is the software equivalent of an ascetic's cave.

Better than either—in fact, better than anything else I've seen—is Dr. Whacko's Stat-O-Mat. My system uses a general-purpose, off-the-shelf database to evaluate the performance of all players across a staggeringly broad range of possibilities. Want to know how a particular batter has done against left-handed pitchers at night? No problem. I think Dr. Whacko's Stat-O-Mat is a triumph of microwave popcorn proportions, but then it ought to be, considering the toll it took on my reputation along the way.

When I began, I had a pencil and a pad of paper. This led to a calculator, and before long I began to explore the possibilities of computerizing softball stats. Because of the limitations of the Macintosh, I decided on a database called Q&A that can be operated on an IBM-compatible laptop. I was ready to go with my new system that spring, but I didn't try to force it down the team's throat. Instead, I started to quietly see if computer analysis could help in a couple of small problem areas, such as the hitting of our sometimes right fielder, Marlon, aka Wonder Bread.

Marlon was an incredibly streaky batter who could just as easily go four-for-four or oh-for-four. I hadn't been able to figure out the problem, so I set it as a test for the computer. First, however, I had to upgrade the quality and detail of our scoring. So I assigned a particular player to be the scorer for each game, and asked him for new information, such as the location of each pitch that was hit, the count on which it was hit, and the field to which each ball was hit. To lessen the burden of the additional work, I decreed free beer (soda, milk, or whatever) for the scorekeeper afterward.

So the information rolled in unobtrusively until, a couple weeks into the season, Marlon's hitting took a nosedive. He couldn't hit the ground if he fell out of an airplane. I had records for a half dozen games at that point, covering both when he was doing well (the first three games) and when he was doing poorly (the last two games). By comparing the two on the computer, I quickly saw some patterns. So I went to Marlon and said. "Look, every time you swing at a high inside pitch you pop it up. Also, it looks like the only time you swing at that kind of pitch is when you are behind in the count. Why don't you try cutting at the first pitch that looks like a strike?"

Marlon nodded with bemusement. He tried it, though, lining the first strike into the gap. That boosted his confidence, and before long he was hotter than ever. Next I talked to Tony. He was easy—I didn't even have to go to the computer to know that His Largeness was a dead-pull hitter who would try to pull his mother if she floated down to him at the plate. He did well when he forced the other team to stop pitching him away by at least occasionally hitting the ball the other way. I told him that, and perhaps because he thought it came from a computer, he followed my advice and began slashing the ball. After that, they came to *me*.

I still wasn't satisfied with the database situation, though. Q&A v. 3.0 had done the job, but it lacked graphics capacity, and I was interested to see how graphing might be able to illuminate certain situations. So I took the plunge on a new database, Reflex v. 2.0, trading Q&A's more advanced word handling for the ability to depict numerical data in a rich array of graphic modes. By the next year, which was the Mouth Breathers' big season, I had switched over to Reflex. I doubt anyone else on the team was aware of the change, though, since the stats all looked the same.

In reality, I couldn't see any significant difference either. I printed out all sorts of pretty pie, bar, line and scatter graphs of the batters' performance, our team run production by inning, and the like, but none of it seemed to reveal anything more than the hard numerical form. Nearly three-quarters of the way through the season, I was on the verge of becoming a chartaphobe when I printed out a graph of the game-by-game offensive production of our infield. Like most graphs, it seemed to show you what you already know, and nothing more.

I could tell at a glance, for instance, that Rod was the big bopper of the infield (and the whole team for that matter), and that Zoomie, Freeman, and Jed followed, in roughly that order. I was about to toss the sheaf in the tottering recycle pile when I was struck by a curious feature of the line on Jed's hitting. From the graph, I could see that he had four very good games during the course of an OK season. I hadn't noticed it before because his good games were so scattered, but here on the graph they stood out clearly.

Investigating further, I found that Jed's really good games had one thing in common. They were all the second game of a doubleheader. I don't know why this was the case. I don't even know if "why" is the correct question to ask in a situation like this. The waters of causality run deep and muddy with chance. (I have a friend who advocates carrying a bomb in your suitcase when you fly because the odds are astronomical against the plane containing *both* your bomb and a terrorist's bomb.)

All I know is the graph showed Jed's power in the second game of the day. Without the computer—and specifically without a program capable of displaying numerical data graphically—I would have missed this. One of the particular strengths of graphs is that they let you quickly scan large chunks of data for exceptional cases, both good and bad. It is also easier for the eye to ascertain the general tendency of a sequence of numbers (so common in Wall Street trendlines) from graphs than from cold figures.

And yet, about 95 percent of the time statistics in any form just seem to confirm what you already know. Some people dismiss them on this basis, but actually it isn't the 95 percent that matters, it's the remaining 5. The value of statistics is their ability to spotlight a player's performance which has escaped the manager's attention. I don't follow the computer's suggestions all the time, but I do look at them because every now and then one of these two-dollar tickets pays off big.

Take Marlon, for instance. He was kind of a walking two-dollar bet. With his scrawny legs and neck, he did not make a very athletic impression, even though an extensive collection of tattoos and scars testified that he had knocked around. In fact, he came from a working-class family where too much money always went to booze, and not enough to food. He grew up on Wonder Bread, Kool-Aid, and Jimmy Dean pork sausage. Once he told me that the first brand-new coat he ever got was when he went to reform school.

Marlon's biggest softball strength was defensive. He had a natural ability to come in on the ball in the outfield. Since right field in slow-pitch generally requires coming in more than going back, I played him in the ten hole, both in the field and at the plate. The big question in my mind when I originally put him in right was whether he would hit enough to justify keeping him there. As it turned out, he hit enough to play the position blindfolded.

Marlon was the one who stepped in and took charge when we were on the verge of losing an important game our big year. We had gotten an incredibly fast start, winning ten of our first twelve games, and coasted on this cushion for more than a month. Then in the last two weeks of the regular season, we were almost over-taken from behind by two teams, the Loggers, who were the reigning champs, and the Merchants, another peren-nial powerhouse. With four games remaining, we had to either beat the Loggers in our last meeting, or win *two* of the remaining three games.

So the last regular-season game against the Loggers was like a championship game for us, since we could walk away with the title if we won. Unfortunately, we resembled the Mouth Breathers of old throughout most of the early innings, blowing leads three times. In the bottom of the seventh we quickly got the tying runs aboard, but then the next two batters went down meekly.

Now we were down to our last out, and who did we have coming up? Our number-ten hitter—the last guy in the batting order. I never thought of pinch-hitting for Marlon, though. He had been hot with the stick, and besides . . . Well, to tell the truth, I was distracted mo-mentarily by the sight of U Jane in the stands behind our dugout.

Marlon was already stepping into the batter's box when I looked back to the game. He fouled off the first pitch. Everybody on both benches leaned forward and clutched their sides with their arms. The next pitch came floating down out of the twilight to fall just a little outside. Ball one.

Everybody on both benches took a deep breath and crossed their legs. One and one. "OK, do it now, Marlon," I thought to myself. Again the ball came floating down and this time Marlon reached out and drilled it down the right-field line for a game-winning three-run home run.

"Wonder Bread!" Rod exclaimed, giving Marlon high-tens at the plate as he scored. Marlon recited Wonder Bread's old "builds strong bodies twelve different ways" jingle in a hiccupy way until we were laughing so hard we were literally falling down.

Living it up to the hilt, Marlon shook, bumped, or fived everybody on the team, except me. When he got to the entrance to the dugout where I was standing, he just reached up and tapped his head with his finger.

DR. WHACKO'S NOTEBOOK

No. 6: Softball Stats

1. The better a team's scorekeeping, the better its manager's decisions are likely to be, since the latter is based on the former.

2. Keeping track of what fields batters hit to (on both teams) is a first step, but keeping track of the count and the location of the pitch can give a manager a finer handle on the individual batter's performance.

3. Even though stats can be kept without a computer program, the keenness of computer analysis cannot be duplicated by casual scrawlings. If you already use a database on a personal computer, see if it can be adapted for softball stat use. The crucial test is usually whether the program has enough relational muscle to perform arithmetic computations on summary fields (i.e., can calculate batting averages).

4. The best programs that I have found for keeping track of softball scores are Q&A and Reflex. Q&A is the more well-rounded of the two, but if you don't already use Q&A or don't need a textual database, Reflex is vastly superior for numerical analysis of any kind. It's available for the Macintosh, too. For a template that will allow you to start keeping your softball records in Q&A, see the appendix.

7

Scared Hairy
by the Montana Terror

The emergency call came around three in the afternoon. I was a little surprised to hear from Bumpy, but not that he was calling from a tavern in Missoula, Montana.

Half-shouting over the din of country western music, he told me he needed help. "It's just too much," he said. "Like those fellas on the Chicago commodity exchange, I'm testing a new bottom."

For nearly a decade, Bumpy had been coach, guiding light, and wet nurse to one of Missoula's most storied softball teams. Called Godswilla, they wore uniforms with an emblem of a winged beer glass on a field of celestial symbols. Beneath it was emblazoned the team's slogan: "A Religion of Convenience."

Nor did the 'Swillas take their vows lightly. They drank before, during, and after their game ("but *not* in the dugout," as they cheerfully pointed out to rule-minded officials). Along the way, they became a force in Missoula's infamous D League, which the same officials will tell you did *not* stand for Drinking League.

Godswilla won the league championship a couple of times, and contended for several more years beyond that.

BRUCE BROWN

Through it all, Bumpy was the catalyst. As the older players retired to the purely religious life at the 8 Ball, he recruited spirited replacements among the young wilders who are always drifting in from the ranches and little towns that dot Montana's outback.

The team's shrine was a plastic garbage can where Bumpy threw his bottle caps, which in those days often had little rebuses printed on the underside. He used to claim he planned to spend his retirement pasting the caps to huge plywood pages, where he would chronicle the glory that was Godswilla in simple drawings and symbols. Lately, though, he had also begun to compile a record of game videos.

Like most people in Missoula, Bumpy was a writer/carpenter by profession. He had originally come to study literature at the University of Montana, but after meeting Beth and fathering Seth and Star, he spent more time with his hands on a hammer than a book. The two things he wouldn't give up were slow-pitch softball and his pony tail, which grew so long he could tuck the end in the back pocket of his jeans.

Everything he did, he did hard. It was his talisman, his ace. Lately, though, it had begun to catch up with him. He had broken his leg snowmobiling without lights one night the previous winter, and the latest bunch of novices was disappointing, as ball players and beer drinkers both. "I sometimes think this goddam team ought to be called Godswilla Lite," Bumpy croaked. "We've lost all our games so far, and tomorrow we face the Weresteer."

Now I understood his anxiety. The Weresteer was another ancient Missoula slow-pitch softball team. It took its name from a horrible creature said to haunt the oldest cemetery in Missoula, located across the street from the Northside softball field. Many times the 'Swillas had been able to beat back the dreaded Weresteer, but they knew them to be a tireless foe, and true to their motto: "Vicious but fair."

"Hope you've got a day game," I ventured cheerfully. Whatever Bumpy said next, I lost in the hubbub behind him as someone began beating on someone else with an aluminum crutch. When Bumpy came back on the line, I suggested all he needed to do was win a couple games in a row, and he'd feel his old spiteful self again.

"It goes deeper than that," he replied. "I need reinforcements." When he mentioned that there was good fishing over in the Bitterroot River right then, I realized that I was being recruited.

"You expect me to fly one thousand miles to play in a D League game in Missoula, Montana?" I asked incredulously.

"Only if you want to," Bumpy answered slyly, adding, "the game's at 7:30. That gives you twenty-eight hours."

"Come on. What about league rules? There's no way you can play me—I'm not on the roster."

"You can impersonate Jimbo, who's going to be vacationing in Spokane."

"But he doesn't have a full beard."

"Exactly! That's why I hope they may think you're him. They've never seen him in a full beard."

"That he grew overnight?" I asked, still not convinced.

Bumpy was slowed a little by that one, but he came back quickly. "We'll say you were scared hairy by the Montana terror."

"Meaning?"

"Meaning a serious job offer," he declared. "In fact, if questioned, we'll present you as a medical marvel."

The flight to Missoula, in case you've never had the pleasure, is a long one from every direction. Then, just as travelers near their destination in the western foothills of the Rockies, they frequently hit the worst weather of the flight. Located at the mouth of Hellgate Canyon, Missoula is buffeted by strong, constantly changing winds.

Bumpy met me at the airport, just like he promised, and took me straight to the Oxford Cafe in downtown Missoula to calm my nerves. The Ox is famous for many things, not the least of which is its breakfast of scrambled eggs and brains, which the leathery short-order waitresses that work the counter announce with a call of "He needs 'em."

"So what's the problem with the Big G?" I asked.

"Same old thing, I guess. Did you ever know Kenny Briggs? They called him Batman—he managed the old Montana Review of Books team one year." I shook my head. "Well, he had an idea he called the Theory of One Bad Inning. He noticed that a lot of time the losing team plays well enough to win—except for one inning when they play horribly and blow it all."

"What was his solution?" I asked.

Bumpy laughed. "Old Batman, he was a crazy fox. He made a rule: As soon as his team committed two errors in a row, he would order the outfielders and infielders to trade places. The third baseman traded with the left fielder, the shortstop with the left-center fielder, etcetera. I saw him do it."

"Did it work?"

"No. It just made things worse. There's a difference between a sieve and a spigot."

I snorted and watched the tattooed crowd milling unsteadily in the glare of the electronic poker machines along the far wall.

"The thing is," Bumpy continued, "we've got the same problem. We play fine—good enough to win even—for five or six innings, and then make a mess of the whole thing with one big, long stinko inning."

"There's a way—" I began.

"I know *that*." Bumpy interrupted. "I've talked myself comatose. I mean, you wouldn't believe what I've gone through to try to get our outfielders to hit their cutoff man on throws into the infield. I've pleaded and begged and threatened. But now I've got them."

While Bumpy drove us out to the field, I changed into Jimbo's shirt. We found the rest of the team gathered along the fence by the visitors' dugout. Most of the players were younger writer/carpenters, but they seemed like decent guys.

Bumpy gathered us all together around one of the light poles. His manner was postmodernist and paternalistic. "Hey, Joey, you'd better get an insulator on that can of beer. . . . No, Fred, this is not Award Night. . . . OK, as some of you may remember, we have not won a game yet this season.

"Some of you may also recall I have been harping about our defensive execution. The phrase cutoff man may ring a bell. On balls to the outfield, we have been throwing the ball all the way to third base trying for runners that we really never had any chance to get, instead of throwing to the cutoff man.

"And then you know what happens? The batter ends up on second base! Then we have no chance for a double play or at least an easy force-out. And on and on it goes.

Before you can scratch yourself, you're down ten runs and packing up to go home.

"How many times," Bumpy asked with a rhetorical flourish, "have I told you to *throw to the cutoff man?*"

One young lad, revealing a marvelously literal turn of mind, answered, "Seventeen, Bumpy, sir."

I saw Bumpy's fingers quivering in front of the bat rack, but he closed them into fists and continued calmly. "My point exactly. You guys never hit the cutoff man. I was telling a friend about it, but he didn't believe me. 'Come on,' he said, 'they've got to hit the cutoff man every once and a while. I mean pure dumb luck would give you that.' "

Bumpy drew himself up ramrod straight, like a Marine defending the flag. "Never," he hissed. "I told him, 'Never.' Well, he still didn't believe it. So he has flown one thousand miles from Or-Egon to see for himself." Pausing momentarily to let the significance of his announcement sink in, he continued, "We have an international observer here monitoring the game. This could lead to recognition in the record book.

"What else have we got here ... oh yes. Don't let Jimbo's sudden and amazing beard growth prevent you from offering your condolences—it seems that he's been offered a job in Rock Springs. I think he's trying to hide. Maybe he thinks that they won't be able to find him behind all those whiskers. Is that you, Jimbo?"

I nodded and spit. "OK, you guys," Bumpy concluded, "let's go lick that cow. Remember, beer is thicker than milk."

On the way onto the field, I heard one guy say to another, "Hey, Oregon isn't in a foreign country, is it?"

"Might as well be," the other answered. "Besides, that guy in left field isn't really Jimbo."

The game began a few minutes before sunset when everyone on the field was washed in peachy light. A nighthawk wheeled across the deepening sky, and off toward the river I thought I heard the whistle of duck wings.

The air seemed to become absolutely clear as the light ebbed. Even way out in left field, I felt I could see the stitches on the ball every pitch. Then they turned on the big ballpark lights, and a cloud of white moths rose to them like snow falling up.

Both teams scored a couple of runs early, and both shut down the other team with some flashy glove-work, the last of which was a diving stab and midair toss back to second base by their shortstop which produced an inning-ending double play.

My big moment came in their half of the inning. After the first batter singled sharply up the middle, the next batter hit a line drive single to left. I motored over, picked up the ball on a couple bounces, and threw it to the short-stop, who had gone out, like a kind of vestigial organ, as the cutoff man. The Weresteers too had apparently heard that the 'Swillas never threw to the cutoff man, so the batter kept coming for second, where he was out easily on the shortstop's relay to the second baseman. We got the next batter to pop out, and the runner on third base—who got there with only one out—did not score.

A couple innings later, the Weresteer reared its ugly head again. They got three more runs, and then with a runner on first, the batter singled hard to left field. However, this time the batter didn't try to stretch it into an automatic double. All it took was one throw! He held at first base, while the man who had been at first scooted around to third base. The next two batters grounded into infield outs, though, so once again they failed to score a runner that got to third.

We came up to bat in the bottom of the seventh inning with the score tied, 9–9. Our opponent had scored some runs, to be sure, but we had not collapsed in a heap, and now the game was ours if we could score one run. Our hotshot shortstop led off with a single. Bumpy strode to the plate next with his favorite wooden bat. He was not an especially powerful hitter, but this time he got ahold of one and cracked a low liner into the gap in left center. The ball hit between the crossing outfielders and skipped past to the wall.

In those days the fences were shorter, around 260 feet, and not particularly tight, resulting in some quirky ground rules. Originally, for instance, any ball that went through or under the fence was a ground-rule double. When it became apparent that some fielders were kicking balls under the fence to call back runners who had already scored, however, the rules were changed to make balls that went through the fence out of bounds, thus giving the base runners an extra base.

Once the ball got by him, the Weresteer's left fielder sprinted to the point where he figured the ball would come off the wall and set himself for the throw to the cutoff man (the shortstop again) who was already in position in shallow left field. Bumpy was churning around first base and our shortstop was sprinting toward third. The intimate confines of the field meant that the ball tended to come back quickly to the outfielders if it stayed in the yard. More than a few runners had bitten the dust on throws from the outfield there, and the crowd in the stands was already rising to its feet.

I saw the numbers on the Weresteer's back—bright red and white against the black mass of the Rockies—and then saw him bend down to field the ball. When he stood up, though, he did not have it. Seeing that the ball had gone through the fence, the umpire motioned the lead runner across the plate, and declared the game concluded.

It happened so fast that the players seemed sort of stunned. Bumpy stopped behind second base, bent over laughing, and put his head between his knees. After a moment or two, the Weresteer fielders began to abandon their positions. Few people left the park, though. Along both foul lines, the two teams began to pull out coolers as soon as the softball gear was stowed.

Figuring that I was less likely to be discovered in the dark, Bumpy climbed up on top of the visitors' dugout and turned off the lights. Suddenly, the stars multiplied breathtakingly, and the party began in earnest. That was the night I first drank beer mixed with tomato juice and heard an impromptu softball satire of *Moby Dick*.

At one point, I asked Bumpy where poet Richard Hugo, who was a great softball player and once published a verse entitled "Missoula Slow-Pitch Tournament," is buried.

He said Hugo's grave was in the old cemetery across the street "under a big tree, out of line with the rest of the graves."

The big Montana night enveloped us, bringing with it a certain sense of the ineffable. I was beginning to feel very tired, and a long way from home. "Must be nice," I said finally.

"I dunno," replied Bumpy, who had obviously done some thinking on the subject. "I want to be buried out there in left-center field where I always try to hit the ball.

"And you know what I want on my tombstone? I want it to read: 'I got it.'"

DR. WHACKO'S NOTEBOOK

No. 7: The Continuing Importance of Defense

1. Batman's basic idea was right. A lot of teams lose because they succumb to the curse of One Bad Inning. What stands between them and winning often isn't a whole new lineup; it's as little as execution on one play in one inning.

2. The only way to prevent big innings is by playing fundamentally sound ball. It is especially important to prevent runners from taking extra bases, which either puts them in scoring position or removes the possibility of a force play for the defense.

3. This means that—among other things—throws from the outfield must go to the cutoff, or relay man. Hitting the cutoff gives the defense a chance to take the ball to any base where a play may exist. Also, it is possible to get the ball all the way home quicker with two sharp throws than with one long, looping heave.

4. Cutoff schemes can get complicated, but in general, the shortstop acts as relay on balls hit to left field; the second baseman acts as relay on balls hit to right field.

8

Catching Heck

Every August the Nooksack Slow-Pitch Softball League holds a championship tournament at Raymond Oliver Park. It's set up so the winner of the regular season gets in free, and all the other teams pay a hundred dollars to see if they can knock them off.

The year the Mouth Breathers won the regular-season pennant, we sensed a certain glee in the eyes of the other teams. Nobody laughed in our faces or anything, but you could tell they thought the pressure would send us scurrying for cover on the sidelines.

Actually, though, we didn't feel any pressure at all. Winning the regular-season pennant was so improbable that we looked on everything else as gravy. None of us was going to be disconsolate if we lost every game in the league championship tournament because we had already exceeded our wildest expectations for the season.

Besides, we weren't planning on losing. I had done a little scouting of the other teams, and I liked what I saw. People usually concentrate on the best players when they scout an opposing team, but not Dr. Whacko. I figure the good players more or less even out at the recreational level. Any team that has a chance of winning has at least a good pitcher, shortstop, left infielder, and first baseman.

To beat this kind of team, you need to exploit a weakness, not assail a strength. That's why I look first at the second baseman, the right fielder, and especially the catcher. When I find a team with an extremely weak catcher, I'm pretty confident the Mouth Breathers have a chance against them. And it's surprising how many teams fall into this category.

You see some real odd catchers. I played on a team once with a guy who was a hundred pounds overweight, wore inch-thick glasses, and liked to read mortuary science texts. We lost him for the season when he tripped on home plate—that's what he said—and fell headlong on his face. He tore up his knee so badly he had to have surgery. There was nobody that bad on the teams we faced in the tournament, but there were some undeniably slow boats.

Of course, a catcher doesn't need to be fast on his feet. Really, he or she must be able to do just one thing. It sounds simple enough, but actually it is one of the most difficult plays in the game, as anyone who has spent time behind the dish can attest. This is to catch a hard throw with a runner coming at you full speed out of the corner of your eye, and then get the tag down in time for the out.

Tony, the Mouth Breathers' backstop, is one of the few catchers I've seen who practices this play. He drills by having someone hit grounders to the infield with a runner on third, who comes hard for home plate on contact. This gives Tony an opportunity to work on the fundamental requirement of the play—keeping his eye on the ball, and not looking at the runner while he catches it—until he is completely comfortable.

By comparison, many recreational-league catchers never encounter a play at the plate until they are in a game with runs on the line. Under this kind of pressure, it's hard enough just to make the play, let alone learn it. As a result, many never pick it up. Their teams essentially concede all plays at the plate, and just hope it doesn't happen very often. It used to be that way with us. You might even say it was a team tradition until Tony showed up.

Another play Tony practiced was catching pop-ups behind the plate. I've heard people say it's impossible to practice this play, but Tony has found a way. He squats down holding the ball behind his back. Then he tosses the ball up with a flip of the wrist. He usually doesn't throw it as high as a real pop, but the action of craning around to sight a ball in the air above is exactly the same as is necessary to catch pop fouls behind the plate.

In time, Tony developed an uncanny ability to snag pop-ups. It was almost as if he could smell the ball, and follow its path as it spun away above the plate. From looking at him, you wouldn't suspect he could get to anything in a hurry, except maybe a piece of cheesecake. He was six feet tall, but the primary impression he gave was width, not height. Squatting down behind the plate, he looked like he intended to set a spell.

I remember looking at the other team's bench one time after Tony grabbed a pop-up. They looked stunned, like they'd seen a mountain hop up and get coffee for their date. Catchable pop-ups occur even less frequently than plays at the plate, but they can make a difference. Over the course of the season, Tony might catch a dozen balls that way, and save a couple of games in the process. And this was just a sidelight to his real strength— taking throws to the plate with a runner coming home.

After watching Tony practice his pop foul routine for a few minutes, a newcomer to the team asked me once why he drilled so relentlessly. "Guilt," I replied. Even though he was a lapsed Catholic, Tony still saw the world in moralistic terms. Guilt and redemption were like the two stones of a bola spinning around an ever-moving center; he might change his profession, even his religion, but he couldn't change what drove him.

Tony had grown up one of seven children in a blue-collar Catholic family on the outskirts of Detroit. He was a choir boy like his two older brothers, but by the time he was thirteen he was already becoming embarrassed by the endless round of bingo nights, pancake breakfasts, and special funds for saints' vestments that seemed to occupy so much of the church's attention. Soon Tony was in trouble pretty much full-time with the Sisters of Mercy at St. Xavietta School.

He actually welcomed the draft notice when it came. After basic training, he was shipped straight to Vietnam, where he saw action in the delta for eleven months. Then he finished out his tour of duty guarding an obscure supply depot in Nassau. "They owed me," he once said. I always got the impression, though, that Vietnam wasn't the real war for him. The real war was in Detroit, because that is where they almost took his soul. Vietnam was horrible, but it also liberated him from the grip of his own past.

I got to know him many years later, after he was hired by the state college to teach philosophy. He soon developed a following among the students for his eccentric attire and irreverent sense of humor. In the wider community, he became known for the house he built on a bluff overlooking the river. It had a tower on one end, and the front half of a decommissioned state ferry on the other. I always suspected he liked the ferry not only because of its whimsy and romance, but also because the doors were double wide.

Since recreational softball rules generally prohibit the catcher physically blocking the plate when a runner is coming home, Tony put his size to another use. "Think of me as the team billboard," he said once, and it wasn't hard to do. Except for the first few innings of important tournament games, he almost never wore the Mouth Breathers regulation uniform shirt. Instead, he favored all sorts of funky T-shirts, most of which bore some sort of slogan or emblem on the back. He sweated so much in the heat that he would change his shirt—and message— several times a game.

He might start out wearing a single word—BREEZE— and follow it with ASK ME WHAT WE DO IN HUMPTULIPS, WASH. Then he might finish with one that was always a particular favorite of mine—WHEN EVOLUTION IS OUTLAWED, ONLY OUTLAWS WILL EVOLVE. Some people on opposing teams thought Tony was an abrasive jerk, but they didn't realize that in a lot of ways he was really on their side. It gets back to the guilt and redemption thing. Tony took each twist and turn of the game as a sort of moral statement, which demanded witness. He was famous among the Mouth Breathers for a play in the final game of the league championship tournament our big year.

He came to bat with runners on base, and our opponent leading by a couple runs. We still had three at-bats—or nine outs—to win the league championship tournament, but I sensed the momentum had shifted. Perhaps we had finally begun to doubt ourselves. It was as if one part of us was waiting to be found out, and banished from the magic kingdom. I was just gearing up to fight resignation when Tony took a called strike three.

The pitch was on the outside corner at the knees. It was a borderline strike, but Tony didn't even wait for the umpire to make the call. He just walked away— conceding the strike, the out, the inning. "Jesus, Tony," I said sourly as he came 'back to the dugout. "You worried about the umpire getting a hernia from having to make all those calls by himself?"

Tony walked to the end of the dugout and picked up his glove. "It was a strike," he said simply. I threw up my hands and headed out to the mound. "What's the deal?" Freeman asked no one in particular as he grabbed his first baseman's glove and a ball for infield warmup. I tugged spasmodically at my beard and muttered, "Saint Tony says it was a strike."

We came back in that game, though, pushing across a lone run in the top half of the last inning on a great piece of clutch hitting by Zoomie. Then in the bottom half, the other team put on a push of its own. They got the tying and winning runs in scoring position with only one out.

The next batter smashed a drive which our shortstop, Rod, took on one hop deep. He threw to first base for the second out, but as the ball left his hand the runner on third headed for home. It was a do-or-die play, with the outcome of the game hanging in the balance. Instantly, our first baseman threw home, bringing ball, glove, and sliding runner all together in a cloud of dust at the plate.

The runner, lying on his back, looked up at the umpire, who pointed his finger at him and hollered, "You're out!" We all jumped two feet in the air, and began to party before we hit the ground.

At the entrance to the dugout, everybody gathered around to congratulate Rod and Tony and trumpet the Mouth Breathers' gasping chant.

"Well . . . ?" Tony asked me at one point in the melee.

"Tony," I said, putting my hand on his vast, oceanic T-shirt, "I don't think we could handle more than one saint on this team."

DR. WHACKO'S NOTEBOOK

No. 8: Slow-Pitch Softball Catching

1. Although often used as a dumping ground for team incompetents, catcher is a very important position which can make a difference in both a game and a season.

2. The most important play for a catcher is taking a hard-thrown ball while a runner is barreling down on the plate and successfully putting down the tag.

3. The best way to master the play at the plate is to practice it. You can do this by having someone hit hard ground balls to the infield, while a runner on third comes home.

4. Another useful (though less crucial) quality in catchers is the ability to catch pop-ups, which can also be practiced by squatting down like the chained hunchback of Notre Dame and lunging at your tormenters all around.

9

The Key That
Turns the Lock

The basic strategic principle of slow-pitch softball is so simple that it can be stated in six words: score runs faster than the opposition.

This may sound idiotically self-evident at first, but think about it. I didn't say score more runs than the opposition, although that is the ultimate goal of the game. I said score them *faster*.

From a strategic point of view, clear sailing in slow-pitch softball goes to the team that is ahead. The leader enjoys the psychological edge of knowing he can score, along with the tactical leeway to play his own particular style of softball.

In fact, the lead is so important that some big-time softball teams, like Steele's Silver Bullets, actually prefer to play as visitors, so they can bat first. They know that a twenty-run top half of the first inning can seriously demoralize the team that bats in the bottom half of the inning. A lot of teams never recover, and are essentially beaten before they even get their first turn at bat.

Steele's main weapon is the homer, but it actually isn't necessary to hit every ball over the fence to score twenty runs an inning. The only real necessity is not making a lot of outs. It all starts with the first batter who hits safely. As Buddha, the legendary sage of Missoula softball, once said: "The rally of one thousand runs begins with a single hit."

And a double is even better than a single. If the principal strategic objective of slow-pitch softball is to score runs as fast as possible, then it follows that having runners in scoring position is crucial to success. This is why doubles are worth more than twice as much as a singles in slow-pitch. Like a good move in chess, a crisp two-bagger simultaneously advances the offense and afflicts the defense.

When a batter doubles, he not only moves into scoring position, he—or she—also puts added pressure on the defense. While infielders often take a deeper position with a runner on second to keep balls from going through for a hit, outfielders tend to cheat in for a throw to the plate. The result is that the defense bunches up, opening holes for a hit to go through that would not be there if the previous hitter either made an out or hit a home run.

But how, you ask, can a double be worth more than a home run? The answer is that although a homer gets you a run immediately, it—like a triple—increases the chances that the next batter will make an out. So the sequence goes something like this: to have the strategic advantage you want to score runs as fast as possible; to score runs as fast as possible you want to get runners into scoring position and avoid making outs; to put runners into scoring position and tilt the odds towards the next person getting a hit, you want to dish up doubles.

The double is the skeleton key that turns all the locks. I remember a game some years ago when I played on a team called the Local Heroes. A sort of all-star squad, the Local Heroes was assembled solely for the purpose of playing a game against a famous touring squad of professionals, the Up 'n' Ups. Sponsored by a Florida chain of high-rise parking garages, the Up 'n' Ups played nearly two hundred games a year on the road, beginning in Texas in late winter and then gradually working their way northward with the seasons' advance.

They got to us in Nooksack, Oregon, on a Wednesday evening in late July. For the Up 'n' Ups it was the third game that week in a swing that was taking them not too directly from Sacramento, California, to Portland, Oregon. The Up 'n' Ups usually played bigger towns than Nooksack, but we got on the schedule because they wanted to break up the drive from Medford to Salem. The management figured they were going to have to spend the night somewhere in Oregon, so they might as well play a game.

I was sitting on the grass under the shade trees that line the road down to the ball field when the Up 'n' Ups pulled in. Watching them pile out of their three custom vans, I was struck immediately by the players' size. They looked like a professional football team. It turned out that their first baseman actually had played fullback in the USFL, and their catcher had wrestled professionally under the name Rock Solid.

They really filled their uniforms, both literally and figuratively. You could see they thought they were studs from the way they loosened up. No simple pepper for them. They honed their swings with a strange chrome object that looked like a robot's leg, and was swung like a bat. No one in Nooksack had ever seen anything like it before, or the aerosol pine tar their leadoff hitter sprayed on his bat just before he stepped up to the plate.

He didn't look much like a leadoff hitter, but then he didn't hit like one, either. He bashed the second pitch I threw at least twenty-five feet over the head of our left fielder for an easy home run. While his teammates congratulated him, I stretched my arms out and flapped like a bird. "Tell the outfield that's the secret signal for 'move back,'" I called to the young buck we had playing shortstop. His eyes widened a bit, but he did motion the outfielders further back into the deepening dusk.

I managed to throw four pitches to the next batter before he hit it out of sight for the Up 'n' Ups' second homer in as many batters. Once again the whole team came out on the field and lined up along the third-base line to congratulate the slugger as he trotted home, flipping high-fives, high-tens, high-ten fingertip flutters followed by butt bounces, forearm bashes, belly bounces, and even an old-fashioned pat on the back or two.

I probably should have been shell-shocked at that point, but I remained sanguine. The wind, which either blows one way or the other in Nooksack, was blowing down the valley at about twenty miles per hour. Because we were playing on a field without fences, we could move the outfielders as far back as we needed. So once again I flapped out behind the mound like an overfed vulture trying to get off the ground.

I figured there had to be some limit to how far they could hit, and for a while it looked like we were conducting an inquiry into just how far that was. Twice more we had to move the outfielders back, but we finally shagged a couple of their long flies, and came back to the dugout in relatively decent shape. Despite nine hits and six home runs, the Up 'n' Ups scored "only" seven runs.

In the home half of the first, it quickly became apparent that the Local Heroes all had firebrands for bats. We batted around, scoring nine runs to take a slim two-run lead. The Up 'n' Ups reclaimed the lead in the top of the second inning on several more booming homers, but the Local Heroes snatched it back again in the bottom half with a clutch of doubles into the gaps.

Unaccustomed to being in a horse race—at least in a town as small as Nooksack—the Up 'n' Ups began to press, both at the plate and in the field. Their pitcher tried to quick-pitch a couple of our hitters in the third, which only succeeded in drawing a warning from the umpire, much to the delight of the roaring crowd. Meanwhile at the plate, the Up 'n' Ups were uppercutting like whiffleball hitters in their effort to drive the ball out of the solar system.

Knowing that local umpires would give me a higher strike than the super-slow-pitch teams are accustomed to seeing, I kept my arc up around twelve feet. Even though good hitters like former major leaguer and current super-slow-pitch star Ted Cox admit that high-arc pitching is hard to hit, most slow-pitch hurlers don't throw high-arc pitches at the super-slow-pitch level. The reason is that pitching up in "the batter's wheelhouse" makes it is easy to drive the ball in the air.

With a twenty-mile-per-hour wind blowing straight in, though, that was exactly what I wanted them to do, so I fed the Up 'n' Ups a steady diet of balls that were either up in the strike zone, or else so ridiculously flat it was nearly impossible to hit them well. They hit some (I remember one pitch on the outside corner that their catcher *pulled* over our left fielder's head), but they also took a lot of called strikes, and pounded a lot of balls up into the wind which ended up falling almost straight down into the hands of our waiting fielders.

Our batters, by comparison, mostly kept the ball down, either on a line or on the ground. The Up 'n' Ups were used to playing on the standard super-slow-pitch field, which has three-hundred-foot fences. Here, though, there were no fences, and they had to cover a lot more ground in the outfield. We began to run 'em, forcing the fielders to weave back and forth to cut off hits. By the fourth inning a couple of their outfielders were tiring noticeably.

The Up 'n' Ups were still a better team in virtually every way, as you would expect from the fact that they were being paid to play the game. Although nominally amateurs, they received money from a variety of sources, including equipment manufacturers, their team's primary sponsor, and local promoter/sponsors like the Nooksack Kiwanis Club, which was putting the whole show on to raise money for a new municipal pool. We managed to stay with them for seven innings because we had a fortuitous combination of doubles, van lag, and wind on our side.

The game finally came down to one at-bat in the last inning. Trailing 32–29 in the top of the seventh, their leadoff batter, the pitcher, did what the good leadoff hitter must do: get on base. He advanced to second on a long fly, and scored on a double. Another fly made it two outs, but the Up 'n' Ups scored again on a huge poke down the right-field line. The hit would have been a homer for almost anyone, but their first baseman only managed to get to third. The score was the Local Heroes 32, Up 'n' Ups 31.

The next batter was their catcher, aka Rock Solid, who had earlier jerked an almost perfect pitch on the outside corner at the knees. By chance, I had seen him before the game talking to a woman with a beehive hairdo and a pendant the size of a cheeseburger around her neck. Although I wasn't sure, I thought I heard them laying a wager on the game. So ol' Rock is a gambler by temperament, I thought to myself.

All the Up 'n' Ups needed to tie the score was a base hit, but I suspected that if I tempted him he would try to win the game with one poke. So I served him a nice-looking pitch up that ran in on his hands just a little at the end. He belted it, but since our outfielders were back (which they probably wouldn't have been with a runner on second), they were able to haul it in for the last out of the game.

I guess it wouldn't be too much of an understatement to say there was one hell of party in Nooksack that night. Worst of all, from the Up 'n' Ups' standpoint, though, was the fact that they had nowhere to go except back to the Harmony Motel, which was crawling with celebrants coming and going from the bar downstairs.

They could have gotten in their vans and been in Eugene before midnight, but instead they decided to just have a beer and some of that marinated steak with all the trimmings. It turned out that they were pretty decent guys. Our right fielder even knew their catcher's brother.

"You think this guy's a ball player, you ought to see his baby brother," our right fielder said. "Tell me, who's Jake playing for these days?"

"Grenville," said Rock.

"Is there a community college there, or what?" our guy asked.

"State pen. The Grenville County Correction Facility. He's doing time for coke. I told him not to mess with that coke, man, but he has a hound's nose for trash."

Later I had a long talk with a couple of the Up 'n' Ups bus drivers, who were probably the happiest people in the pros' entourage since they did not have to drive that night.

One of them told me that the Up 'n' Ups' catcher "lost five hundred dollars that last at-bat, you know. He had at least that much riding on our winning."

"Why'd he do it, then?" I asked, a little too drunk to be anything but direct. "I mean, all he had to do was single up the middle to get the tie. That would have been easy with a pitch like that. Why did he go for the game-winning homer?"

The driver, who was bald and not at all athletic-looking, leaned back in his chair reflectively. "The names and the faces change," he said finally, "but the egos remain the same."

DR. WHACKO'S NOTEBOOK
No. 9: Overall Offensive Strategy

1. The basic strategic principle of slow-pitch softball can be stated simply: Score runs faster than the opposition. Or, put another way: Good things happen to those who have the lead.

2. It is not necessary to hit tons of home runs to score tons of runs. To score runs faster than the opposition, all you really have to do is put runners in scoring position and avoid outs.

3. The double is the most valuable hit in slow-pitch softball because it specifically addresses these needs. It puts a runner in scoring position, eliminates the force or double play, and in most situations causes the defense to bunch up, making it easier for the next batter to both drive in a run and avoid making an out.

4. A lot of batters think their job is done when they get to first. In reality, they should be thinking double all the way, and scanning the field as they round the bag for a sign—such as the outfielder's bobbling the ball—that they can make it. Not everybody can hit homers, but just about everybody can hit doubles if they work at it.

10

Land of a Thousand Pitches

Remember how I urged pitchers to concentrate on one pitch, and simplify their motion to the plate? Well, now we've come to the part where I contradict what I said before.

It's true that sticking with a single pitch and a consistent windup can help a person learn control. But it's also true that one pitch is not enough to win in competitive slow-pitch, even if you can throw it between your legs.

At the highest level of slow-pitch, the hurlers usually have three, four, and even five pitches in their repertoire. A curve, screwball, and knuckleball are the most common, but you also see an occasional palmball, dropball, and slider.

Because the mechanics of pitching are much less standardized in slow-pitch than in baseball, the style of delivery varies wildly. One of the largest slow-pitch organizations, the U.S.S.S.A., even allows pitchers to bounce the ball off their foot. The best pitchers can also deliver pitches which break more than one way from the same motion, and the same apparent spin.

It's like in baseball, where you often see a pitcher throw two kinds of fastballs, one of which tails away from a hitter, and one of which rides up and in on him. Neither breaks a great deal—at least compared to a curve or screwball—but because they are thrown with identical motion and spin, they can deceive a hitter enough to throw off his timing and make him hit the ball off a weak part of the bat.

If the other team is any good—and there is enough light for the batter to find the plate—you are not going to blow anybody away in slow-pitch. That's why the best major league analogue to a good softball pitcher is not Sandy Koufax or Bob Gibson or Nolan Ryan. It is somebody like Luis Tiant or Whitey Ford or Gaylord Perry in his last years when he had nothing left but guile and guts. It is John Tudor striking out Kent Hrbek with a slow curve in the 1987 World Series.

In both baseball and slow-pitch softball, the secret to making the ball move in and out is the grip. Take the simple backspin pitch that is the most common offering at lower levels of the game. If you hold the ball with the seams, so that your finger tips are touching the place where the seams loop over like a duck's bill, the ball will track pretty true and straight in light air, or drift with a stronger wind. However, if you hold the ball across the seams—with the "duck bill" between your thumb and forefinger—it will cut from right to left from a right-handed pitcher. In light air, this pitch moves a little like a conventional curve, and in a breeze it can track straight, countering the effects of the wind.

You can get some feeling for how a backspin pitch will move in the air from a child's gyroscope. If you spin a gyroscope and then suspend it so that its axis is horizontal like a softball, instead of vertical like a globe, you can quickly grasp the gyroscopic force exerted on the pitch. Interestingly, the spin maintains the ball's equilibrium and resists twisting in most circumstances, but not all. There are certain occasions—especially when the axis of the ball's spin is not perpendicular to the arc of its flight—when gyroscopic spin actually causes the ball to move in the air, rolling in the characteristic wobble that scientists call gyroscopic precession. This sort of movement is responsible for both the global advance of the seasons and the liveliest backspin pitches.

Sidespin pitching is something else entirely, since the spin here often works more like a corkscrew than a gyroscope. A little harder to throw because the sighting and control are a little less direct, sidespin pitching is nonetheless employed by most better pitchers to some extent. One reason is that the ball breaks better with a sidespin delivery. It is possible to throw a really effective curve with sidespin. When I die, I'm sure one of the memories that flashes before my eyes will be of a sunny afternoon when I struck out twice in a row on slow curves, both of which were thrown inside, and then broke down to catch the corner of the plate.

Rolled off the fingers (and sometimes palm) as the pitcher's hand comes up, sidespin is more of a "touch" pitch, requiring a more complex series of coordinated body motions. It can take more practice to master with consistent accuracy, and more practice to maintain an edge. The flip side of the coin is that sidespin deliveries tend to be easier on the arm. I've found personally that this means I am less likely to tense up in pressure situations with a sidespin pitch than with a backspin pitch. It is also possible to vary the arc and speed of sidespin offerings better than backspin, multiplying one pitch into two or three or four.

Even so, sidespin pitching isn't what you'd call over-powering. The only pitch that can be truly hard to hit in slow-pitch softball is the knuckleball. Sometimes when it is in mid-air, a player will call a warning from the dugout, "knuckler," as if it was a German U-boat. By this, they mean a pitch with little or no spin. Lacking the envelope of spinning air and accompanying gyroscopic effects to stabilize its flight, the knuckler can veer suddenly with slight changes in the air currents over the plate. I have seen a knuckleball break as much as a foot in the last few feet of its fall to the plate.

Despite what you might think from the name, you don't use your knuckles to throw the knuckleball. In fact, most knuckleballers grip the ball with their fingernails (so that the fleshy parts of their fingers don't touch the ball at all), and delicately launch it into the air as if they were floating saucers on a pond. You need big hands to throw the knuckler this way, but some people with smaller hands have managed to throw another kind of knuckler by gripping the ball deep in their hand, much like a palmball and releasing it with a sort of underhanded putt.

The best knuckleballer I ever played with was called Eighter. He had large hands, but what most people noticed first about him was his compulsiveness. He came to pitch the way a person who is addicted to gambling comes to the casino. While some of us were there to goof off and have fun, he was there because he *needed* to be. Listening to him one day, it occurred to me that the knuckleball breeds fatalism because luck—in the form of the wind—plays a greater role with this pitch than any other. Knuckleballers have got to have what they can't control.

Going back to Eddie Cicotte, the Chicago "Black Sox" ace, fate has marked many knuckleballers with mixed blessings. The baffling effectiveness of the pitch seems to have had a souring effect on some of the people who have thrown it. This is particularly evident in the career of Burt Hooton, the knuckle-curver extraordinaire. He threw a no-hitter against the Cuban National Team as a twenty-one-year-old amateur, went undefeated as a major league rookie with the Chicago Cubs, and later starred in several World Series for the Los Angeles Dodgers, but he was rarely seen smiling in public.

Eighter could smile, although it didn't really make you feel too good. Warming him up before games, I learned it was best not to bother him until he had gauged the wind. To do this, he would set up for his warm-ups so that he was parallel with the mound on the actual playing field, not the foul lines or fences. He was the first pitcher I ever saw who did that, and he did it every time because he knew he was going to live or die by what the wind did to his offering.

Experience proved he was likely to be in a good mood if there was a light to moderate quartering wind. His favorite trick was to throw the ball when the wind had gusted up a little and was somewhat steady, then have the breeze die away as the ball was falling to the batter. If he could catch that moment with any consistency, he could be truly horrible to hit against. I've seen good hitters swing and miss two swings out of three, and go back to the bench thankful that they managed to ground out to the second baseman.

Of course, there were lots of times when the wind wasn't just right or when Eighter couldn't control the snake he was wrestling with enough to throw strikes. Then he could be a wild presence on the mound. I remember a game in Spandee years ago when we were both playing for a team sponsored by a health-food deli called the Gnoshers. The team was made up of some of the restaurant's biggest customers, several waiters who also worked summer stock in Ashland and elsewhere on the southern Oregon theater circuit, and some normal folks like Eighter and yours truly.

Unfortunately, Eighter's mound performance that evening was like six acts of Sophocles, with the rest of the infield cast as the Greek chorus. After our opposition scored four runs and re-loaded the bases with nobody out, the infield gathered around Eighter on the mound. He immediately suggested they wave their arms when he started his windup.

"Why?" the infield asked in chorus.

"Boy, sometimes I wonder about you guys. To create a backdraft, of course! I need a backdraft to make the knuckler do a real love dance."

"Uh, Eighter, I dunno," somebody said. "Maybe it would help if we all breathed in at the same time, too."

"Gosh," Eighter said, his eyes growing even wider, "that's a great idea. Let's do it. When I'm ready, I'll give the signal, and everybody wave their arms and breathe in . . ."

"Hold everything," the chorus advised. "A soothsayer approaches."

"Well, Big Boy," Willie, our manager, said as he joined the discussion on the mound, "we're gonna need some grease to get through this squeeze."

"Who falsely wins, all sacred things profaning," the chorus chimed in, "shall he escape the punishment of his doomed pride?"

"Stop it!" the manager yelled. "I told you not to do that. It's creepy."

"Good words," the chorus came back, "and fitting for a prudent man to hear and heed. Quick thoughts, though sure, are seldom safest . . ."

"You heard me," the manager bellowed. "Do you guys get together and practice that stuff or something?"

One of us started to speak, but another one stepped on his foot. Apparently satisfied that he had at least taken care of that problem, Willie turned back to Eighter. "OK, what's going on out here?"

"We were talking about breathing," Eighter said. Then he described his back-wind scheme to Willie, who listened for about three seconds before flying into another rage.

"Correct me if I'm wrong," he shouted, "but we're playing softball, right?"

"Check."

"Well, then, let's get on with it."

"You boys still interested in playing?" the umpire asked, joining the group on the mound.

"An omen in blue . . ."

"I beg your pardon?"

"Let's go, you guys," Willie growled like he meant it.

So the infielders all retreated to their places around the diamond. Eighter tucked the ball in his glove and squinted in at our catcher, as if there was any doubt what he was going to throw. Everybody there knew it was going to be a knuckleball. What they couldn't tell you was how it was going to break. He stared some more, then backed off the mound.

When he came back, there was fire in his eyes. Rocking into his motion, he delivered a pitch that immediately vanished into a tiny speck in the distance. It was a grand-slam homer, and the game was as good as over.

I turned and walked toward the outfield grass while the runners circled the bases. "Well, what do you make of that?" our second baseman asked as he joined me.

"It's possible to be a winning pitcher with just one hand," I said, "but not one pitch."

DR. WHACKO'S NOTEBOOK

No. 10: Advanced Pitching Styles

1. Advanced pitchers are able to throw both a variety of pitches and pitches that move differently from the same motion and apparent spin.

2. As in baseball, the grip is the key to making the ball move in and out. With backspin pitching, you can make it move differently by throwing it with, or across, the seams.

3. Sidespin pitching is a little harder to master, but is much more mutable than backspin, and therefore can add several pitches to the pitcher's repertoire.

4. The knuckleball is the only pitch in slow-pitch softball that can be overpowering. It is thrown with a sort of stiff-wristed putt—and poot—off the fingernails. The idea is to release the ball with no spin. If the pitcher's hand is too small, a similar pitch can be thrown by holding the ball in the palm.

11

How I Hit .000
in Havana

The big black Soviet limousine rolled heavily in the turns as we sped through Havana in the early evening. Riding in the back seat, I flopped from side to side between my two bulky companions.

They were both dressed in slacks and pale pastel guayabera shirts with tiny pleats and pearl buttons. One was clean-shaven and cradled a trim leather attaché, while the other was mustachioed and smoked an unfiltered cigarette.

"A little early sliding practice?" I asked as we bumped together for the dozenth time. The man with the attaché translated my comment into idiomatic Spanish, even though I knew the other man spoke excellent, softly inflected English.

"We don't want to be late," the man with the moustache replied with a slight smile. Then he added something else in Spanish to the driver, who nodded and steered us off the large downtown boulevards into the older working-class residential areas on the east side of the city.

Driving with the windows open, I could smell a pungent mix of hibiscus and fried palm oil. The traffic thinned, but we were stopped twice by young boys playing baseball in the street who would not let the car pass until they were through.

It was nearly 7:30 P.M. when we arrived at a ball field set in the midst of a colorful jumble of somewhat seedy houses. We parked behind the grandstand, which was built of concrete and brick and looked solid enough to withstand a direct rocket attack. After the man with the moustache, whose name was Barbaro, had removed a khaki duffel from the trunk of the big black car, we went into the bowels of the stadium.

There we were shown into a dressing room. I took off my tourist togs and donned an all-new softball uniform, with Cuban manufactured jersey, pants, stirrup socks, and even spikes and gloves, all straight out of the box. Each bore the insignia of the Cuban sports equipment concern *Batos*, which takes its name from the ball and stick game played by Cuban Indians when the first Spanish explorers encountered them in the fifteenth century. My uniform pants were dark blue with a thin red and blue stripe up the side, while both my socks and shirt were red. Emblazoned across the chest in blue was the word *Desporte*, Spanish for *sport*.

I took an extra long look at myself in the mirror before going down the runway to the field because it was all a little hard to believe. For the previous two weeks I had been travelling in Nicaragua on the Baseballs Not Bombs program. We were giving away American baseball equipment in an effort to foster international goodwill through love of baseball. During my group's two weeks in Nicaragua, we visited dozens of towns and played a little *pelota* ourselves in several of them. Now I was trying to figure out who in Nicaragua had set me up for this little Cuban detour.

My flight home was booked ahead of time on an Air Canada flight to Vancouver, B.C., which made a stop in Havana. Soon after we touched down at Jose Marti International Airport, some of us were asked to show our passports. I was the only United States citizen on the flight, and the one they seemed interested in. When the Cuban inspector saw my American passport with the proudly embossed eagle, he asked me to get my carry-on baggage and accompany him. I protested that I was just a tourist. I may have even said something about my mother worrying if I got home late.

It didn't do any good. Two more uniformed Cuban officers poked their heads through the doorway of the plane, and there was some murmuring among the flight crew forward. We all sat there for another ten minutes or so until it became apparent that nobody was going to move unless I did. So I finally got up and followed the officers out of the plane. Walking across the hot, steaming tarmac in the early Havana evening, I was struck by the airport's bustling international mix of aircraft and airlines. The impression was a brief one, though, for I was quickly ushered into a first-floor interrogation room.

There I found myself face to face with a tall, mustachioed man with an easy air of authority. He said he believed he knew something about me, adding, "I want to warn you—we view this as a very serious matter." Then he cracked a smile and asked, "Would you like to play a little softball?" I replied that I'd love to, but added regretfully that I had no equipment with me, not even a pair of tennis shoes. *"No hay problema,"* Barbaro said.

BRUCE BROWN

"We want to see for ourselves this crazy physician of the baseball."

Four hours later, I found myself playing second base for the Ministry of Sport. Most of my teammates worked for the Ministry of Sport, and their locker-room banter about the job and various personalities from the office was immediately recognizable to anyone who has played on a company softball team in the U.S. In fact, the whole scene reminded me of the urban recreational leagues in America, with the exception that the Cuban facilities were better. Few American public park facilities provide dressing rooms, and many do not have dugouts.

Warming up on the sidelines before the game, I was surprised to see that the covered grandstand was over half full. Fifteen minutes before the game there were already several hundred men, women, and children lounging in the shade and jabbering between sips of colas and coffees. It was here that I first glimpsed our opponents stretching on the other side of the field. They wore midnight blue uniforms with the word *Propaganda* in yellow on their shirts. When I asked Barbaro what that meant, he replied that the other team represented the Ministry of Propaganda. "The Ministry of Sport against the Ministry of Propaganda. It is a moral contest, no?"

Replying that virtue was clearly on our side, I inquired about the other team's personnel. "They have a good quick infield, and a decent outfield," Barbaro said as we tossed a ball back and forth on the sidelines. "One guy, their regular right fielder, played baseball for the Havana team in the *Series Nacional.* He's left-handed, and a dead-pull hitter. The best player on their team is the pitcher, though. He is that fellow over there, the paunchy one.

His name is Raoul, and he has been at the game for a long time. When he was sixteen he ran away from home to join Che Guevara's column. During the fighting for Santiago de Cuba, he is said to have once lobbed a grenade into the open turret hatch of a tank. Now he just tosses softballs, but he is still feared by his opponents."

Studying him from the dugout during the top half of the first inning, I could see that Raoul had an unusual—perhaps even eccentric—style. Before each pitch, he held the ball up for the batter to inspect, as if it were some sort of a holy orb or object of profound reverence. I didn't detect anything particularly impressive about his stuff, except that our half of the inning was over before Barbaro could get his cigarette lit. It took Raoul a grand total of five pitches to retire the side, and although one ball was hit pretty hard, the right fielder was there to make an easy catch.

I faced him for the first time in the third, with one on and one out. While I dug myself a place in the batter's box, he took the throw from his shortstop, walked off to the side of the mound with his back to me, and then turned and toed the rubber. His expression as he gazed in at me was mild and almost friendly as he held up the ball for me to inspect. It was as if he was saying, "See, here it is. Hit it if you can." I thought to myself, "Thank you very much," and I lashed an outside pitch hard on a line—straight into the hands of the second baseman.

Back out on the field, I pondered the international differences in the game. Cuban slow-pitch allows the pitcher a great deal more latitude in terms of his motion and the speed of the pitch. He can break rhythm—à la Satchel Paige's "hesitation pitch"—as well as throw faster, relatively flat pitches that would not be allowed in the

United States. The effect is still the same—it's still impossible for the pitcher to overwhelm the batter—but there is room for more cunning. Compared to the many varieties of American slow-pitch, the Cuban game is closer to United States Slow-Pitch Softball Association rules than the more widespread Amateur Softball Association rules.

That evening in Havana, the Ministry of Propaganda scored three more runs to take a five-run lead under darkening skies. It had been hot and sunny less than two hours before, but now the late afternoon filled with broken clouds which sent dramatic shafts of sunlight plunging to the surface of Havana Bay and the golden-green water of the Caribbean beyond. By game time the clouds began to thicken overhead, promising rain. The big banks of lights were turned on at the ball field in the fifth inning, and soon silent lightning flickered in the clouds. Before the end of the inning, the first drops began to fall, buzzing in the red clay dust like flies in a spider's web. The rain increased until it raised a din on the metal roof of the grandstand, and then passed as quickly as it had come.

The air had a clean, cool feeling of home when I came up again in the fifth inning. The two batters before me had singled, showing that Raoul could be reached. They stood on first and second as I watched the pitcher go through his ritual. I felt relaxed and confident enough to look for a particular pitch. Since I had gone the opposite way the first time up, I thought he might try to pitch me inside. I decided I'd look for an inside pitch to pull. The first pitch fell over the inside corner of the plate. It would have been a strike, but I drilled a long line drive that the left fielder took on the run at the fence along the foul line. A lot of times a hit like that would go for extra bases, but not this time.

I got my only fielding opportunity the next inning—a grounder to my right—and handled it flawlessly. Otherwise, however, things did not go well. The flashy right fielder for the Ministry of Propaganda belted a huge two-run homer, and they went on to win by a score of 7–2. Showering in the dressing room afterward, Barbaro did not seem deeply saddened by the outcome, though. "Another victory for propaganda," he commented matter-of-factly as we hurried to get out of the way for the team playing the next game.

Back at the car, we found the driver listening to a Miami radio station on the Soviet-made radio, but he quickly turned it off and got out to open the trunk for Barbaro's duffel. This time Barbaro and I rode alone in the back, for the translator had been excused for the rest of the evening.

"You are hitting the ball well," he said as the car pulled away.

"Not well enough," I replied.

Barbaro paused as we passed a Fiat on the left. "The key to hitting Raoul," Barbara continued, "is understanding what he is doing with his windup."

"You mean that silly bit where he holds up the ball?"

"No, that is just show. The thing you have to watch is what he does before. You see how he always walks to the rubber from one side of the mound or the other. The direction he comes to the rubber from is a signal to the rest of his team. That's how he tells them whether the next pitch is going to be inside or outside.

"The defense behind him always knows where the pitch is going to be, and so where the ball is likely to be hit. The fielders are careful not to move too soon and give it away. But you'll see that they are in motion as the pitch leaves his hand."

"Well, what's the point of holding the ball up like some sort of grail?"

"Have you ever studied magic?"

"*Lo siento*?" I said, beginning to feel a little strange.

"I'm not talking about witchcraft, but illusionism. The magician always presents something obvious for popular scrutiny, but actually the real business takes place elsewhere, while people's attention is distracted."

Barbaro looked at me out of the corner of his eye and blew a lazy cloud of smoke, adding, "There are also several obvious analogies to U.S. foreign policy."

At that moment we vaulted over an unlit railroad track, and I was flung into his lap.

DR. WHACKO'S NOTEBOOK

No. 11: Coordinating the Pitcher and the Defense

1. One of the simplest ways to increase the effectiveness of a pitcher is to have the defense positioned correctly for the pitches thrown.

2. Once a pitcher has gained sufficient control to be able to put the ball where he or she wants it more than half the time, it's important to set up a system of signals to inform the fielders where the ball is going to be pitched.

3. The signals can be given either by the pitcher directly, as in the case of Raoul's theatrical chicanery, or by a second person such as the catcher or shortstop. The only requirement is that they be visible to everyone on the field, yet not obviously a signal.

4. It is equally important that the fielders—especially the infielders—not tip off the batter by breaking too soon. If they wait until the pitch is in the air, and then break correctly (to their right if the ball is inside to a right-handed hitter; to their left if it's outside to the same batter), they will catch a lot of balls that normally would go through for hits.

12

Wrong Place, Right Time

"Well, this is it," I thought to myself. "I should try to remember what it feels like."

Somewhere behind me, I heard raucous laughter. Shifting in my lawn chair, I could see little clouds of dust rising from the infield where the grounds crew was preparing for the last game.

Beyond, a group of young boys were chasing each other around the concession stand, while a young woman in tight red shorts was walking slowly up the grandstand stairs with two sodas.

Just like two weekends before at the league championship tournament, the Mouth Breathers had skated through to the final round. We had won three games on Saturday, and then we had beaten a pretty good beer team first thing on Sunday morning.

That got us into the final game, which was played at 3:00 Sunday afternoon. By 2:30 I figured there were already at least a hundred people in the stands. They'd come from as far away as Polk and even Wilburton to see the Loggers meet the Mouth Breathers in a rematch for the softball championship of Nooksack County.

Largely composed of friends and relatives of the players, the crowd was knowledgeable and—when the opportunity presented itself—loud. Also, there were always a

couple plans afoot for some sort of high jinks, like the
time the Elmo boys blocked the river bridge by parking
their father's bunting-bedecked log skidder crossways in
the middle.

"What a food line!" Zoomie exclaimed as he sank into
the chair beside me with a paper bag in his hand.

"Did you get my onion burger with the works?" I
asked.

"Well, not exactly."

"What do you mean, 'Not exactly'? How 'not exactly'?"

Zoomie rummaged in the bag, and handed me something that was long and thin.

"This is a corn dog," I protested. "And not only that,
it's a naked corn dog. Couldn't you at least have gotten
some ketchup or mustard?"

"The line was horrible, man," he said between bites of
nachos. "I was lucky to get this stuff."

I took a bite of the corn dog and rewrapped it. "Hey,
Dog Breath," I called, "you want a slightly used corn dog?"

"Sure," Tony replied predictably.

"So what's the lineup this time, Cap?" asked Jed.

"I was just about to figure that out," I replied, wiping
my hands on my uniform pants and pulling out the scorebook. Almost instinctively I wrote the first four names:

Zoomie (2nd)
Boo (rt center)
Dr. Whacko (1st)
Rod (ss)

All four could hit for average or power, as the situation demanded. Equally important from the standpoint
of slow-pitch softball, the first three batters were also

fleet base runners, who were likely to score if the chance presented itself. Rod, by comparison, was a true power hitter who was accustomed to doing his scoring on the trot. Then I wrote:

Jed (3rd)
Steve (lft)
Sol (lft center)

Normally Steve, our left fielder, batted fifth behind Rod, but this time I decided to try something different. Remembering the computer's tip that Jed excelled in doubleheaders, I decided to bat him fifth. Steve, who was actually a better hitter than Jed, batted next. His presence would discourage the Loggers from pitching around Jed, and the same was true of the man who batted behind him, Sol.

Sometimes known as "The Wall," Sol was a strapping farm boy in his early thirties. About all I knew about him was that he lived on the family dairy with his ailing mother. He joined us partway through the season and soon made a mark by playing *hard*.

The bottom of the batting order took longer than the rest, even though there was less choice. Chewing on the corners of my moustache, I considered the angles. Finally, I settled on:

St. Tony (catch)
Freeman (pitch)
Wonder Bread (rt)

I wanted Tony, who often batted higher in the order, to protect Sol. Freeman might do the same for Tony, but actually my reason for batting Freeman so low in the order was to allow him to concentrate on pitching.

This was probably the biggest change I made going into the championship game. I had pitched the majority of our games that season (including all but one of the five games we'd played so far in the league championship tournament), and I think everyone expected me to pitch the finale.

I just had a hunch. During the regular season, I'd faced the Loggers three times, and beaten them twice. The Loggers came on strong at the end of the season, though, and I felt they were catching up with me. Freeman had only pitched a couple games since his big no-hitter, but I knew he could be dominating in spot starts.

So I decided to give him the ball, and hope that the Loggers' relative unfamiliarity with his looping style would give us the boost we needed—because it was obvious to just about everyone in the by-now packed house that we were going to need something extra if we were going to prevail. I don't know exactly what odds you could get in the men's lavatory, but the Loggers were heavy favorites.

And it made sense. The Loggers were historically the strongest team in our league, having won the championship two of the last four years. They were big and strong, and boasted some marvelous players, including Pick Webster, who was probably the best outfielder in the league, and definitely the one you wanted to pick if you were fortunate enough to have the choice.

Another factor in the Loggers' favor was the fact they had "been there before," as the sports cliché puts it, while we had never even been in the same zip code with the championship before. I was worried about the first inning, but I needn't have been. Freeman got in the groove, and the contest proved a taut, seesaw affair that saw the lead change hands every inning until the sixth when we came up leading, 17–15. Since I had made the last out the previous inning, Rod led off and promptly doubled into the gap in left.

Jed, who had done nothing at all to that point, followed with a double into the gap the other way. Having been stung two times in a row, the Loggers' outfielders took a couple steps back as Steve, whom they knew and respected, came up to bat. This was fortunate for us, since Steve hit a looping little flair that fell just beyond the Loggers' lurching shortstop and cued away down the left-field foul line.

When the dust cleared, Steve was on second with our third double in a row, and we now led by four, 19–15. Because there were no outs and the runner on second could not be forced (love those doubles!), the Loggers' manager, Chet Willis, was forced to gamble. Sensing that the game was on the verge of slipping out of reach with only one at-bat remaining, Chet called Pick Webster in from the outfield to play behind second base as a fifth infielder.

"Great," Zoomie said to me on the bench at the time, "that's like Hitler using the Messerschmitt Me 262 to bomb London." Actually, there is considerable debate about the virtues and liabilities of special defensive alignments. In coed ball, fielders routinely shift back and forth between male and female batters (although the introduction of a smaller ball for the women's at-bats in some leagues has begun to change this). I have also seen some of the best men's teams in slow-pitch softball—including Steele's Silver Bullets—go into radical defensive shifts.

Generally, though, shifts in alignment work best on a limited batter who is well known to the defensive team. The bell curve of success falls off steeply on one side as the batter gets better, and on the other as the defensive team's knowledge of the hitter diminishes. There is no doubt that the standard alignment of four outfielders across is superior, on the average, to any other. But there are also times when using one outfielder as a rover or extra infielder can steal what would have been a hit. There is also an element of uncertainty because, as with an on-side kick in football, you never know exactly what's going to happen.

Sometimes a batter will be distracted by the ploy and essentially take himself out. Sometimes making base runners think about one more thing is all it takes to short-circuit their brains and make them wander off base like a snow-blind penguin. Of course, it can work the other way, too. The Loggers were betting that we couldn't handle it. With the game in the balance, they were gambling that they could prevent us from scoring any more runs by drawing Pick in to a position about twenty feet behind second base. It would be impossible for Steve to score on anything that Pick flagged, even if it went for a hit.

I know Chet pretty well because he works on my car at 'Sack Service. He's got a real shrewd sense of where in a mechanism a loose bolt is hiding. I've seen him go into a baler and extract a sheared pin like a surgeon removing a tumor. This time, though, he might have done better to change pitchers, because the next batter, Sol, hit the ball harder than anyone so far. It was a high, towering shot that fell between the Loggers' racing (but depleted) outfielders. Sol is not very fast, but he could see this one was extra bases, so he put his head down and poured on the gas.

He looked almost comic as he churned toward second like a piece of self-propelled architecture, but I knew there was another side to Sol. I remember one sunny morning at the beginning of batting practice not too long after he joined the team. A lot of the guys were still stretching and getting out their gear. The second or third pitch I threw Sol was outside about waist high. With an explosive grunt, he crushed the ball straight at my face. I got the leather up and caught the ball—but just barely. After that, all Sol's flashes of hostility were directed toward our opponents.

So when Sol came steaming around second base and saw Pick standing in the base path, I wasn't surprised when he didn't hesitate or veer. Unfortunately, Pick was not only out of position and in the base path, he was also half turned for the throw from the outfield that he was never going to catch. Sol, who was once a red-shirt linebacker for the University of Oregon Ducks, hit Pick from the blindside with a flying forearm that knocked him head over heels onto the grass at the edge of the outfield.

Everyone in the stands could see immediately that Sol had iced Pick. The Loggers rushed to his limp form in the grass, oblivious to the ball bouncing weakly across the infield as Sol came home. We scored it a two-run homer, but the Loggers angrily disagreed. They argued that Sol should be evicted from the game for unsportsmanlike conduct, and Steve be ordered out of the dugout and back to third base. In the stands, the largely pro-Loggers crowd began raining ice cubes from their drinks and other debris down on the field.

After Pick finally got up and started walking around on the grass rubbing his head, the umpire, Fred Rollins, called me out of the dugout to talk to Chet and him. Chet, who was madder than I have ever seen him, was already in full cry. "I have never seen a dirtier play than that one," he yelled at something like the top of his lungs. "Do you realize that my player could have been seriously injured? Do you want to talk about the cost of insurance for this league if you tolerate this sort of garbage?"

Sensing an infinitesimal pause, I jumped in, for I believe in the Hydrostatic Pressure Principle in arguments with umpires. That is, to preserve equilibrium you need to apply equal pressure on both sides. "Nobody wants to see Pick or anybody else get hurt," I screamed. "But Chet, he was in the base path. Your man was in the base path, and the best way to keep him from getting hurt is to keep him out of the runner's way! If you want to talk about rule violations, your man should be called for interference."

"Look, I've played this game for nearly twenty years," Chet began before the umpire cut him off. "The runner is entitled to the base path," the umpire intoned. "Both runners score, and there are no outs." To me he continued, "I want to make it clear, though, that I will not tolerate any violence on this field. I'm warning you now, and I want you to tell your football player there: If I see any unnecessary roughness from anyone, they're gone. Is that clear?" I nodded and meekly mumbled my assent. "OK, let's play ball!"

Pick stayed in the game, but Chet brought in a new pitcher. Tony greeted him with a hit, and Zoomie and Boo delivered back-to-back RBI doubles before I made the final out of the inning again. And so the Mouth Breathers took a 23–15 lead into the game's last frame. A comfortable margin? Not in football or slow-pitch softball. There was no telling how the Loggers would react to the incident with Sol and Pick. It could either fire them up, or kick in all their tent stakes.

The Loggers got four runs back in the top of the seventh to make the score 23–19, but they gave up two outs in the process. Then Freeman, who was working effortlessly as clear water flowing over a smooth rock, got two strikes on Chet's assistant at the garage, Freddie. Never known as a selective hitter, Freddie lashed the next pitch to Rod at short, who gloved it and fired across to yours truly for the last out, the victory, and the league tournament championship.

Coming on the heels of our regular-season championship, there was no doubt that we had established ourselves as the best team around—for the moment. We were all ecstatic, of course, and hardly noticed the dark mood of the majority of the crowd who had bet on the Loggers. For us, it was what you would call a dream come true, except for the fact that I don't think any of us ever dreamed that we would win the double crown in our league that year.

I was especially proud of the fact it was a team effort. Everyone had made a contribution, with the possible exception of yours truly. In fact, you could almost say that we had won because of the things that I didn't do more than because of things I did do. For instance, my not pitching was crucial, as was my not indulging in defensive gambles. Perhaps my contribution was catching Rod's last throw.

As soon as we could get away, we all adjourned to Pete's Tap for a full-scale celebration. It was the first time that many of us had ever been anything like local celebrities, at least in any positive sort of way. We were still toasting our own heroics when a sheriff's deputy came in.

The deputy scanned the room, and began to make his way over to our table. I saw him lean over and speak to Sol, who stood up and followed the officer between the tightly packed tables toward the door.

Feeling a residual sense of responsibility, I ran after them to see what was happening. Outside, I heard the deputy tell Sol that someone had set fire to his calf shed.

I could tell this wasn't the real news the deputy brought, though. The officer took off his hat and told Sol that his mother had had a heart attack.

"Where is she now?" Sol asked, half demanding, half imploring.

"It's OK, son," he said. "She's safe."

But we knew from the way he said it that she was dead.

DR. WHACKO'S NOTEBOOK
No. 12: Defensive Shifts

1. The strongest defensive alignment is usually straight away, with all four outfielders spread evenly.

2. There are certain exceptions, however, where the correct defensive shift can work well. In general, defensive shifts work best against a limited batter who is well known to the defense.

3. Even teams at the highest level of slow-pitch will sometimes employ a radical shift (such as bringing an outfielder in to play as a fifth infielder) to try to shake things up, and introduce an element of chance.

4. Just when it all begins to seem too complicated for any mortal to master, remember that paunchy men with chewing tobacco running down their chins can do it, and so can you. If you're lucky, like me, the things you don't do may be crucial to success.

13

If You Can't Stand
the Heat . . .

The main difference between men's softball and coed softball is that coed is harder. That's right—playing with women is more demanding than playing with men alone.

This is partly due to different coed rules, which put two people on base when a man walks (but not when a woman walks). The idea is to prevent a team from pitching around the other team's men, which is a good idea, but it puts much more pressure on the pitcher.

Certainly I've felt the additional pressure of knowing that four balls were worth the same as two singles. It isn't the sort of thing I like to brag about, but I suppose I might as well tell you myself before you hear it from someone else. I once stormed off the field screaming in the middle of a coed slow-pitch game in Nooksack, and only came back long enough to hurl my glove into the stands.

This unfortunate performance was set up by a series of miscues that prominently included my walking back-to-back men, and thus loading the bases for the other team and giving them a run gratis. I came apart like a cheap suitcase in the rain after we muffed a play that could have gotten us out of the inning. I'd induced the batter to hit a slow dribbler down the first-base line, which I fielded myself and tossed to Stephanie, our first baseman.

It was an easy underhand lob, but because the first baseman's eyes flickered for a moment to the runner hurtling down the line, the ball dropped out of the end of her glove. Passing by her on my way back to the mound, I made the mistake of saying, "You've got to keep your eye on the ball." Stephanie didn't say anything back, but when I got to the mound, I sensed a deep chill in the air.

Looking around, I saw Stephanie standing at her position with tears running down her face and her shoulders silently heaving up and down. Meanwhile, the other women in the infield were looking armor-piercing shells at me. The expressions on their faces told me that I was in deep trouble with them—trouble deeper than the game—for giving Stephanie an accurate appraisal of the situation, or at least that's the way it seemed to me.

In retrospect, I'd say it's better to have these episodes by yourself in the middle of the night. But I couldn't help myself. I just flipped. Now, years later, I think the whole incident had less to do with softball rules than the underlying differences in male and female culture. Like most American males, I absorbed some rough idea of the jock code while I was growing up. Although hard to fully articulate because of its essentially guttural nature, one of the code's principal features is the idea that if you get knocked down, you don't cry, you just keep getting up and coming back until you get it right.

Implicit in this is the idea that learning to deal with adversity in general is as important as learning the particular skill in question. As boys, we were taught that it was not disgraceful to miss a ball, but it *was* disgraceful not to make a game try. This had been among the fundamental rules of conduct governing ball-field behavior all my life. The sun had risen and set, I had gotten first better, then older, the uniforms and sponsors changed, but the jock code remained immutable. I accepted it the way I accepted the fact the grass was green and the diamond had four bases.

Which is to say, I never gave it a moment's thought until years later when a woman who was playing second base on a coed team missed a grounder. She wasn't a particularly good infielder because she was really still afraid of the ball. So the male coach who was hitting infield practice said, "Let's do it again, Marcia." She made a game try, but the ball skipped off her knee, convincing her that her original impulse to avoid the ball was correct. Picking up another ball, the coach said, "One more time, Marcia." She didn't really try for that one, and so he hit her another even faster.

Before you could read the defendant his rights, Marcia threw herself down in the dirt sobbing, and all the other women on the team gathered around her. "Well, I hope you're satisfied now, MISTER," one of the women said, as she put her arm around Marcia. The men on the team stood transfixed, as if a UFO had landed on the edge of the outfield grass. The whole thing was a bolt out of a blue sky for us, for we really had not intended to hurt or humiliate Marcia. We were trying to help her! But we soon learned that the women didn't see it that way.

Rather than isolate the problem player and test her, the women wanted to support and encourage her through positive reinforcement. This was their group ethos. I don't know if they teach girls this sort of thing in

Brownies the way they teach the jock code to boys in Little League, but I am certain of this: Any male player who doesn't make allowance for it is going to come to grief in coed softball. Many women find the jock code barbaric, and simply don't recognize its authority any more than Palestinians recognize Israel.

The best coed teams have developed their own hybridized way of doing things, which brings the best of each sex to the diamond. Such teams are often exceptionally strong units, and can actually beat all-male teams that you'd think were superior when you looked at them on paper. I learned a lot about these dynamics from watching good coed squads, but the thing I liked best about coed softball was getting to know women like Karen Singletary as friends.

Karen was the town librarian, and generally looked the part, with small features and a quiet demeanor. If you knew her casually you would probably think she was nice and bland, but you'd be wrong, at least about the latter. Actually, Karen was a prolific and almost totally private poet. She wrote hundreds of poems that no one ever saw unless they dropped by unexpectedly. I remember seeing one attached to her refrigerator with magnets once.

It was a striking little meditation on the white frost shadows you see under trees on clear cold mornings. I couldn't do justice to it here, but it made think about something beautiful I'd really never focused on before, and briefly put it in the perspective of the cosmos.

"Extra! Extra!" Karen deadpanned when she saw me reading the poem. "Sun Goes Down, Comes Up."

"It's still news," Ted, her husband, said.

"The best I know," I added.

Karen had a way of sneaking up on people. I remember a public forum that was held at the library a few years ago. The main speaker was a county councilman who was under pressure to account for certain road department expenditures.

Several people pressed him on the issue when it came to the question-and-answer period. Finally, a little defensively, he said, "You act like I buried the money in my front yard."

Quicker than a deer over a cattle fence, Karen asked in her proper little voice, "Where did you bury it?"

On the softball field, Karen showed the same gutsiness. Once on a hot August day she lost a high fly ball in the sun, but she didn't budge an inch. She stayed with the ball, staring up into the blinding blue sky for some sign of the falling ball until it hit her right in the eye.

It sounds funny now, but we were all scared half to death at the time. Her eye swelled up immediately and took on the ugly, yellow-tinged look of a bad bruise. Later, we heard that some people who didn't know she played softball wondered if her husband had beaten her.

I myself wondered considerably more about Karen. "Most people have enough natural cowardice to get out of the way of a ball like that," I told her. "What's the matter with you?"

"Librarians know no fear," she declared.

"I guess not. Just watch out it isn't a steel safe next time."

I played shortstop in that long-ago time, and so it was my responsibility to take throws to second base from the right side of the outfield, where Karen usually played. At first, I came off the bag and cheated up into the shallow outfield when I saw a ball hit to her. The reason, I guess, was that she was a woman, and a rather slight one at that.

She quickly put me in my place, though, which was on the corner of the bag. That's where her throws were most of the time if they weren't cut off. She didn't have the blazing raw athleticism I've seen in some women, but she got the job done. And not only that, she got better. While the average male player her age was slowly but irrevocably deteriorating, she was becoming a markedly stronger player.

I remember a game at Raymond Oliver Park against a team with a real hotdog center fielder. He was a fast left-handed slap hitter who routinely took an extra base against women. He lined a single into right and tried for a double—having gotten away with it on Karen every time we'd played them up until then. This time, though, she was running in fast when she caught the ball. Using her momentum, she got off a surprisingly hard peg that proved to be right on the mark, and nailed the dude by a stride.

He was a little upset about getting his uniform dirty for just an out. I knew how he felt, though. The best shortstop I personally ever played against was a young Indian woman named Sharon Tenmile. An exceptional athlete, she stood five foot six inches tall and weighed 120 pounds when I first met her. Once, at a tournament in Nooksack, I hit a hard line drive about four inches in front of her on the backhand side. This is one of the toughest of all plays. She was up to it, though, deftly short-hopping the ball and throwing me out with ease.

Her play was such a thing of beauty that I hardly minded being out. She had shown us a flash of major league leather and proved just how well softball can be played in America's small towns. I was particularly impressed because I knew I couldn't have made the play. So I began to follow the career of Sharon Tenmile. The next time we played the Umpquish Indian team, she had put on at least twenty pounds, becoming a slugging third baseman. Within a few more years, she had ballooned into a lumbering catcher with awesome, powerful looking thighs and butt.

After that, she only played an inning here or there, as her weight climbed up over three hundred pounds, and she raised eight or nine kids of her own, plus a couple of her husband's from a previous marriage. She still had the pretty face of the teenager who amazed me with her glove-work not too many years before, but otherwise she was unrecognizable. She could really block the plate with the best of them, though. Once in a game on the tribal field overlooking the mud flats of Umpquish Bay, Sharon prevented a run from scoring by *sitting* on home plate.

The runner came dashing home and ran by in front of the umpire. About halfway to her team's dugout, though, she realized she hadn't ever touched the plate. Spinning around, she hurried to where it was supposed to be, but she couldn't find it. A look of desperate terror crossed her face until she realized what Sharon was doing. The runner was just turning to complain to the umpire when the throw came in from the relay man in short left field. Now Sharon was standing on top of the plate with the ball in her hand. After a long moment, the two women threw their arms around each other and laughed until they cried.

Another reason that some men have trouble playing softball with women is that they are more important to the coed game than the men are. This is partly the result of the way the coed game is structured. It is generally pretty easy to find five decent male softball players, but finding five strong female players is something else. Since the men even out, the women hold the balance of most coed games in their sway. Some women players are just better than their male counterparts, too. Karen and Sharon leap to mind, but the most outstanding example I've ever known is U Jane.

In the heat of the action on the field, when the ball is flying back and forth and the fate of the game is on the line, U Jane has an uncanny ability to focus on the crucial part of the chaotic picture. She always knows where the ball is, and where the next play must be made. It's as if she can study the whole thing from somewhere above the fray. I once saw a copy of *A Practical Guide to Astral Projection* in her bag, but I really don't think out-of-body experiences explain U Jane's savvy on the diamond. Quite the contrary!

She has a way of snatching the advantage right out of the other teams' pockets. When the other team begins to string together some hits, they often become aggressive to the point of recklessness on the base paths. Then U Jane is like a hawk. You hear her sing out "second" or "home" as soon as she detects a careless runner who may be vulnerable to a snap throw.

When U Jane is on the mound, plays that began with the other team getting a hit and perhaps even scoring a run often end with an out. Like the big curve she throws, she has the capacity to take situations that have wandered astray and bend them back—for a strike, or an out, or a friend.

DR. WHACKO'S NOTEBOOK
No. 13: Coed Softball

1. Coed softball is another realm entirely from the men's game, and in many ways I think it's harder.

2. Rule changes intended to even up men and women—such as playing with different-sized balls, and attaching penalties to walking men—change the basic geometry of the game. An inadvertant result of this is that the pitcher's task is made much more difficult.

3. Women are more important to winning at slow-pitch softball than men, both because of the rule changes and because the men more or less even out, putting a premium on the superior woman player.

4. If you're alert (and heaven knows, the world needs more lerts), you can sometimes snatch victory from the jaws of defeat by keeping your eyes peeled for runners who carelessly round bases too widely in the heat of the fray. The pitcher is usually responsible for making the defensive call, but many—men and women alike—don't even know it's an option.

14

Both Ends
of the Stick

We drove to Eugene in four cars the night before the subregional tournament and stayed in the No Tell Motel.

It was as if they'd built a palace with us in mind. There was an all-night quick market next door, and we were impressed by the establishment's thoughtful touches, like ashtrays in the showers.

Boo found a paper shoe polishing strip with the slogan "Our guests are king for their stay," and promenaded from room to room with it hung off his mohawk like some sort of bizarre Christmas ornament.

He got a couple laughs, but mostly the Mouth Breathers seemed to have their minds on bed. In fact, most of us were a little nervous. One hundred miles was the farthest we'd ever traveled as a team, and this tournament was the toughest challenge we'd faced. Some of us had never seen this level of tournament softball, let alone *played* in it.

Another cause for concern was the fact that we were missing two important players from the lineup that took the Nooksack County championship. One was Sol, who never played with the Mouth Breathers again. This was bound to hurt since Sol had provided the spark in our big win three weeks before, but even more damaging was Rod's absence.

Rod was crucial to the team on both defense—where he played shortstop—and offense—where he batted cleanup. He wasn't an instigator of our trademark antics, but he was the one who made the most difference in the team's play. We called ourselves Dr. Whacko and the Mouth Breathers, but we probably should have been called Rod and the Rodettes.

Most of the team didn't hear about Rod until we were leaving for Eugene. Several guys were obviously dismayed, especially when they learned that he had gone to a tribal ceremony in the Willowas for a kid he had never actually met. "I rescheduled my trip to San Francisco so he can go wear leather pants in Pendleton?" complained Boo. "And what about these new uniforms?" Tony asked me. "What'd they cost you, Doc?"

I shrugged, even though I could have told him the figure. I had no idea why Rod chose that moment to split, but I did know that it's hard to be a solid citizen in both the Indian and white worlds. Even trying to avoid the Indian's myriad family obligations can be a full-time job, and then there are the special ceremonies. A pillar of the Indian community may be compelled to spend his entire life savings to throw a big party to pass on an ancient family name, which makes it hard to play the bond market at the same time.

Rod was caught in this conflict, among others. Like a mote of dust quivering in the air between two electromagnetic fields, he was driven back and forth without ever attaining either side. He never became the tribal leader or college professor or major league shortstop that various people at various times hoped he would. On the surface, little seemed to distinguish the semisqualor of his life from that of other Indians in the area. He had one obvious ability that life had not been able to knock out of him, though.

Rod was a great natural hitter. There was a sound that the ball often made leaving his bat that was unlike any other I ever heard, even though lots of people used the same bat. The sharp report and rocketing hiss reminded me a little of incoming artillery fire. Rod hit the ball well almost every time, but he was not a contact hitter by any stretch of the imagination. He was a true slugger, and the only legitimate power threat on our team. We had several people with gap power and good speed, but he was the only one who routinely hit them far enough so he could trot around the bases.

Looking at him, it was immediately apparent why. He was overbuilt. He looked like he came from a world where gravity was twice as strong as it is on earth. His arms and legs seemed bowed from a lifetime of resisting a force that was pressing him down. He was more than strong, though. When the situation demanded a long ball, Rod knew how to tilt his sights up a little, and hit just a hair below the middle of the ball to make it carry. This gives the ball backspin, and lofts it like a high iron shot in golf. All the famous professional slow-pitch softball power hitters use this stroke, but you have to be strong to get away with it. Otherwise it's just another long fly to the outfield.

Rod liked to cut the sleeves off his uniform shirts, à la Ted Kluszewski on the Cincinnati Reds in the 1950s, to show off his glistening brown shoulders. He also usually wore gym shorts over knee-length electric red Lycra tights with black chevrons up the sides. Lots of people thought he was just being a hotdog Indian, but once again, things were not exactly what they seemed. Now it's certainly true that Rod was capable of hotdogging on the field, but I knew he wore the tights because they covered the scar of an ugly Vietnam shrapnel wound.

If you spent a season or more with him, you would notice that he was quicker moving to his right than his left at shortstop. He compensated by cheating to the left, and almost daring you to hit it by him in the hole. A lot of people tried, and a lot of people were nailed at first. With his great one-way range, quick reflexes, and sure hands and excellent arm, Rod was actually a better-than-average shortstop. He also added a certain headiness under fire, saving us more than once by astutely being in position to flag a throw that got away. Then there was his hitting, which was really ferocious: he led the team in batting average, slugging percentage, home runs, total bases, and RBI that year.

I don't know, but I think what made Rod a feared hitter had as much to do with his dreams as his mechanics at the plate. Rod's half brother, Willy John, told me that Rod had been having the same dream ever since he got back to the States from 'Nam. It was a small-scale, personal sort of thing. There were no roaring gunships annihilating hillsides at a stroke in his dream. There was just an old woman coming around the corner of her house. She had gray hair and a black apron on. Over hundreds of repetitions, Rod strained to preserve the woman in that last moment before she exploded into bloody meat beneath the M-16, and he awoke in a jungle sweat.

Rod's wife, Elaine, and their kids absorbed some of his confusion and anger. They were a family where the kids were always explaining to school officials that they got their black eye running into a door. Rod's fleet of semiderelict cars took some more of the abuse. His main outlet, though, was probably slow-pitch softball. I used to wonder how the guy could be such a good hitter, and finally I decided it was that he was completely relaxed. Softball was a place where his demons couldn't pursue him. It was one place where never missing was a blessing, not a curse.

Rod played, and started, in every Mouth Breathers game but one that year. Often Elaine with a couple of the kids came to cheer the team on, too. The kids' wild Indian whoops (there's nothing like the real thing, you know) were a constant refrain that summer. I remember one time they jumped right up on top of the scorer's table when Rod hit a big homer for us. You might say Rod's family put their mark on the game in more ways than one. The kids often sat on the bench with the team, too, and literally fought for the honor of getting Rod's bat for him. Elaine eventually took over the crucial scoring chores because she and the kids were such regulars.

The only indication I had beforehand that Rod might not make the subregionals was when he said about a week before in a kind of vague way, almost as if he was talking to himself, "I got to go to a secret society ceremony in the Willowas." No sense of time, or urgency. No sense of connection, or warning. I guess I should have read Rod's smoke signals, but I was as surprised as the rest when I swung by his house on my way in to rendezvous for the drive to Eugene, and found that nobody was home but Buddy, the family's mongrel dog. Finally I thought to call Willy John, and he told me where Rod and the family had gone.

Without him, the rest of the team looked as scrawny as a wet cat. We were scheduled to start at 8:00 A.M. in the first subregional game of the day against Willamette Screw and Nut, a perennial powerhouse. I dropped myself into the cleanup slot in place of Rod, but it didn't make much difference because we went one-two-three in the first inning, so the number-four batter didn't even get to the plate. When we made three outs in a row again in the second inning, I began to fear the effects of some global condition like El Niño was causing a previously undetected deadening effect in aluminum bats.

The problem with my theory—to say nothing of the game—was that this aforementioned power outage only seemed to affect one side of the diamond. The Screws were not having any trouble getting the ball to jump, with six homers through the first two innings. A couple of these homers were exceptionally robust specimens, the kind where the ball doesn't come back until a couple minutes after the batter has crossed home plate. It got so bad in the third inning that the game was delayed for lack of balls. They'd hit the umpire's whole supply into the long grass, and we had to wait until the outfielders and grounds crew could find them.

Meanwhile, the Mouth Breathers were unable to scratch together more than a couple of singles in one inning. I should give the Screws' pitcher credit—he was sharp, especially when he got ahead on the count. He had a trick that Chicago softball legend Ed Zolna used, too. Sometimes when he was delivering the ball he'd step toward the third-base foul line, instead of the plate. This meant that a few times during the course of the game, the batters faced a totally different motion which concealed the ball much longer, and brought it from a different angle. He got two of us—including yours truly—to foul out with that maneuver.

Really, though, the problem was that we were just plain bad. After travelling a hundred miles to the tournament, we were out by 8:30 A.M. on the first day. They ten-runned us, 18–2, and the umpire called the game after five innings. The whole thing happened so fast that most of us were kind of dazed. We shuffled—or maybe slunk would be a better word for it—out of the dugout to make way for the next team, and threw ourselves on the grass by the river.

"Losing's bad enough," Zoomie said, finally breaking the ice, "but beer doesn't even taste good at this time of day."

"What are we supposed to do?" asked Tony. "Meditate on our sins until sundown?"

"I'll crack," Boo said. "I'll never be able to take it."

"I think what we're supposed to do now is go home," I said.

"Spend money," Tony corrected me, "and *then* go home."

"Check. Uh, Steve, you got any money left to spend? How about you, Jed? I don't even need to ask you," I added, nodding at Marvin.

"I've got money for a six-pack," Wonder Bread declared defensively.

"Well, I guess we're ready to go."

Then in the distance we saw a group of figures approaching. There was a woman and several kids and a man whose heavy-set power was evident from halfway across the field. It was Rod and Elaine and the kids. Rod was wearing his uniform and Elaine had her scorebook under her arm.

It turned out that they had driven all night after the ceremony was over in the Willowas to get to Eugene that morning. "I thought I could trust you to win one game," Rod said a little flatly.

Now it was we who found ourselves apologizing.

Finally we piled back into the cars, and headed down I-5 toward Nooksack. It was hot by ten in the morning. Rolling down the windows, we let the August wind wash us with the sweet scent of hay and hops.

After a while, it was no longer too early to drink beer. Then Boo hung the paper he had taken from the motel on the rearview mirror of his old root beer–colored Pontiac.

I watched it waving "Our visitors are king for their stay" at the empty road behind, and felt better with each passing mile.

DR. WHACKO'S NOTEBOOK
No. 14: The Power Stroke

1. At the highest levels of slow-pitch softball, power hitting is perhaps the most important aspect of the game. You often hear people scoff at softball sluggers as beer-bellied dreamers, but actually the slow-pitch softball stroke is a special enough thing that even big-league hitters have to learn it.

2. Ted Cox, who played in the American League for the Cleveland Indians, Boston Red Sox, Seattle Mariners, and Toronto Blue Jays, told me that the basic trick to power hitting in slow-pitch softball is to strike the ball slightly below the middle, in order to give the ball backspin and loft it. "In baseball you are taught to hit the top part of the ball. Now you slow your hands down so you make contact, and then snap the wrists to get the spin to make it carry."

3. When the power game is on, it can be absolutely overpowering. I watched a game in the 1989 ASA super-slow-pitch national championships in which one team, Steele's Silver Bullets, hit fifty-six homers, winning by a final score of 74–21. It is worth noting, though, that Steele's didn't win the super-slow-pitch national championship that year. They were beaten by a team that featured speed and an all-around game.

15

Snow Ball

I probably should have had enough sense to let the softball season end there in Eugene. Somehow I just couldn't quit like that, though. That's why I signed us up for the annual "snow ball" tournament played every winter in the Oregon mountains.

I've got to admit that the Mouth Breathers didn't all share my enthusiasm. A couple players already had plans for the holidays, and a couple more obviously thought I had finally crossed some sort of invisible line on the subject of slow-pitch softball.

Summoning all of my wiles, however, I was able to talk, cajole, blackmail, chauffeur, and otherwise collect eleven guys for the drive up to a frozen mountain lake on the Saturday after Christmas. There were Zoomie, Boo, Tony, Jed, and me, plus six ringers, including Tony's seventeen-year-old stepson.

Our destination was Lake We Hi Um, located just over three thousand feet above sea level in the Cascades. The main road to Bend skirts its shore for several miles on the east side of the summit of We Hi Um Pass, allowing year-round access.

Nestled in the cold shadow of a formidable array of peaks and hanging glaciers, Lake We Hi Um had been icebound since November. This made it possible for the tournament officials to get the diamonds set up early.

Now, however, the whole affair was undoubtedly disappearing beneath the snow that had been falling in the mountains all night. We saw oncoming cars that were pasted with snow before we got to Mosquito, but I didn't bother to put on chains when the flashing amber lights at the state highway department barn warned of hazardous snow conditions ahead.

We continued on in silence until I nearly went broadside in front of an oncoming truck trying to get out of the way of a stalled Pinto. Then someone in the back seat said, with an attempt at casualness, "Say, I wonder if they'll even hold this thing? I mean the road doesn't look too good. You think maybe we'd be better off going back?"

"Yeah," another voice quickly took up the theme, "we might be the only ones there."

"That's exactly why I want to keep going," I said, hitting the gas to get around another car, which had stopped in the middle of the road to put on chains. "I figure we've got a good chance to collect some forfeit victories here. Who knows, if we *are* the only ones who got through, we could win it all. I mean, who else could they give the trophy to?"

When we steered our rented eleven-passenger van into the parking lot at the lake a half hour later, though, we found we were not alone. A half-dozen teams were already "warming up." The sight of them gathered around the trunks of their cars and playing catch was familiar to anyone who has played softball, but the sense of familiarity ended as soon as we looked at the playing fields.

At first all we could see in the sea of white were the fluorescent orange traffic cones that were being used as bases. Then the details began to emerge, like the fact that only the infields had been swept down to clean ice. The outfield—and everything else—was covered with a foot or more of new-fallen snow, which was crisscrossed with the tracks of the fielders, snow hares, and lost skiers.

"Wow, the ultimate honky ball," Zoomie said.

It took about two tosses apiece for us to put all our normal white balls back in the bag, and stick to the one homemade orange one Boo brought. The white ones literally vanished the moment they left the thrower's hand, and were dangerous. Nobody wanted to stand around too much, so we got started right away against a team from Roseburg called the Wasted Knights.

Zoomie was the first batter. Because of the cold, perhaps, he swung at the first pitch and lined it to right field. Watching him made me think of how Ed Zolna tells hitters who wanted to go the other way to "hit the inside corner of the ball," or the side of the ball that faces the batter as it falls.

This is exactly the place that Minnesota Fats would strike with the cue ball if softball were billiards. It's also another way of telling the batter to wait, because you can't hit the "inside corner" of the ball until it has descended well over the plate (and, not coincidentally, into the meat of most batters' power zone, if they are positioned correctly in the batter's box).

I began to bask in a glowing sense of immutable softball verities. All normal softball thoughts vanished, however, when Zoomie's ball hit the snow about twenty feet beyond the second baseman and disappeared. Normally a hit like this would have been a single, but now as Wasted Knights searched desperately a few feet away, Zoomie rounded second and headed for third base at top speed.

Too late, he remembered that he wasn't on dirt, locked his brakes, and slid past third base standing up like a surfer. Then at the last second, he reached out and grabbed the orange cone, knocking both of them over. He and the base continued for some distance, finally coming to rest in deep snow. Meantime, the Wasted Knights found the ball and relayed it in. Zoomie just laughed, though. "Hey, I got the base," he said when the man came to tag him with the ball.

We soon found that any ball hit to the outfield was subject to strangeness in the air and on the ground. For instance, in the second inning one of their guys hit a ball to right center. Boo slogged over and dove for the ball at the last instant. We saw the ball hit his mitt just before he vanished beneath the snow. For a long moment, he was gone. Then he stood up about a dozen feet away from where we'd seen him disappear. He still had the ball, along with a nose full of snow.

Balls on the infield were a whole different matter. Here, where the soft snow had been cleared, the surface was quicksilver fast but generally true. The unusual thing about infield grounders was the sound. Whenever a hard grounder was hit, the clear ice underneath rang like a huge water chime, producing some beautiful sounds that I never would have dreamed could have come from a simple five-three groundout.

In the swirling snow, bare skin quickly burned a lobster-red color. Spirits remained pretty high, though. Every inning when we came in to the bench, Boo jammed his red hand in one of those round insulated holders that are supposed to keep your beer cool.

At the start of the third inning, I took myself out and put Tony in to pitch. "You don't want to be seen on the same field with us?" Tony asked.

"No, I don't think you need me," I replied.

The snow stopped falling after a while, and the clouds drew back enough to reveal the dramatic faces of the surrounding cliffs. I saw the pink blur of a finch in the tall Douglas firs on the other side of the parking lot, and wondered if it was drawn by the musical sound of our grounders.

As my mind wandered further afield, I thought of U Jane. And not for the first time, either. While the out-fielders searched for another lost ball, I imagined her in my high-school gym class. For some reason, we were doing a rope drill that must have been a school board requirement, because everybody had to spend one day a semester on the ropes. Basically, the idea was to swing on these hawsers from station to station around the gym.

I had just gotten to the third station and was awaiting my turn to move on when this girl came swinging in on the rope and landed right in front of me. She had gray eyes and long freckled legs. "Me Tarzan," she said with a laugh as she handed me the rope.

"You Jane!" I cried out of my dream, compulsively completing the venerable line.

"Yes?" I heard a voice at my side say.

Turning around, I saw U Jane standing in the snow beside the bench.

"You look kind of odd," she said. "Is something wrong?"

"I'm fine," I lied. "But what are you doing here?"

"I thought I'd find you at the snow ball tournament," she said, although I wasn't sure she was replying to my question.

"Well, no sacrifice is too great for softball."

We chatted for a couple minutes before U Jane asked, "Did you know there is a hot springs near here?"

"Seriously?"

"Umm-hmm. It's just around the lake shore a ways and back up a canyon a little bit."

"Where's this?" I asked, perhaps a trifle too quickly.

"Come on, I'll show you," she said indulgently, taking my hand and slipping it in the warm pocket of her coat.

The last thing I remember of the game was hearing Tony say, "Does anybody know what the score is?"

DR. WHACKO'S NOTEBOOK

No. 15: A Few More Things

1. One way to seriously hit to the opposite field (right field for a right-handed batter) is to try to hit the "inside corner of the ball." That is, waiting long enough on the pitch so you can hit an inside slice of the ball as it falls through the strike zone.

2. Less seriously, softball in the snow can be great fun as long as you don't expect it to resemble dry-land softball too much. If you want to try it, you'll need orange balls, and orange traffic cones or rubber tires may serve as better bases than the bags used during the summer. It also helps to have some sort of warming shed. Major snow ball tournaments have been sponsored for many winters in Omaha and Chicago by the March of Dimes.

3. Although it may not happen often, you occasionally may want to do something besides play softball. (Did I say that?) Just remember the lines from the eighteenth-century British poet William Cowper: "Absence of occupation is not rest, a mind quite vacant is a mind distress'd."

Appendix

Excuse me a second, I'll just close this door. OK, now that there's nobody here except computer people, I want to say a couple things about flat-file databases and softball stats.

In the first place, I am not a complete fan of either Borland's Reflex or Symantec's Q&A for a variety of reasons, both large and small.

For instance, Q&A insists on displaying all decimal fractions with a leading zero. This means that batting averages look like 0.279 instead of .279.

In addition, Q&A has limits on its sorting capabilities which make it impossible to list players by batting average, from best to worst. Reflex has similar sorting limitations, and lacks any macro capacity, making it unsuitable for many repetitive tasks.

Still, Reflex v. 2.0 and Q&A v. 3.0 will get the basic job done. Their design and output are generally superior to programs dedicated specially to baseball statistics, and when you're through you can use them for other purposes, too.

If you're one of the hundreds of thousands people who already use Q&A or Reflex, you should really try keeping your softball stats with them. Chances are, they will show you things you never dreamed of about your team, and the game in general.

So here are step-by-step directions for setting up a database in Q&A to keep softball, baseball, or Rotisserie ball statistics. In addition to keeping track of basic stats like batting average, total bases, etc., Dr. Whacko's Stat-O-Mat allows you to compare the contributions of widely divergent types of players.

By means of the Whacko Points, you can examine the relative value of sluggers and singles hitters, or even hitters and pitchers. Whacko Points also make it possible to get an idea of the total contribution of hitting pitchers, who are of course the rule in slow-pitch softball.

As much fun as the following codes and equations sound, I realize that some people may prefer to avoid doing it all by hand themselves. For information about softball and baseball stat files preloaded on disk for Q&A and Reflex, write:

Dr. Whacko's Stat-O-Mat
P.O. Box 393
Sumas, WA 98295

In the following template, I will deal quickly with general aspects of Q&A that experienced users will already know, and new users can look up in the manual. My most detailed comments will deal with the equations and codes specifically required to set up a softball scoring system. So here we go.

Open Q&A, and at the main menu, choose F for File. At the main File menu, choose D for Design file, then D for Design a new file. Name the file (softball, perhaps?). At the blank field screen, type each of the following field names, followed by a colon, in any arrangement you like. Then once you have finished and are presented with the field type screen, go back through and add the following capital letter codes (Q&A's default is T for text):

```
last name: T
first name: T
position: N
relief pitcher: Y
team: T
league: T
start: Y
team: T
against: T
at: T
date: N
week #: N
night: Y
pitcher: T
lefty: Y
1B: N
2B: N
3B: N
HR: N
RBI: N
RUNS: N
SB: N
E: N
HITS: N
AB: N
Tot. AB: N
Tot. Bases: N
Tot. Bat. Pts.: N
INN PIT: N
EAR RUN: N
```

```
COMP GAME: N
ShO: N
WIN: N
LOSS: N
SAVE: N
HITS: N
WALKS: N
HBP: N
Inn. Pts.: N
ERA Pts.: N
Bonus Pts.: N
Tot. Pit. Pts.: N
WHACKO POINTS: N
```

You should be able to arrange these fields on one page of the blank Q&A form without too much trouble. Now drop down to the second page of the form layout and type:

```
in.sub1: N
in.sub2: N
in.sub3: N
in.sub4: N
in.sub5: N
in.sub6: N
in.sub7: N
in.sub8: N
in.sub9: N
er.sub1: N
er.sub2: N
er.sub3: N
er.sub4: N
er.sub5: N
er.sub6: N
```

```
er.sub7: N
er.sub8: N
er.sub9: N
bo.sub1: N
```

Because the last set of fields are located on the second page, they are normally hidden when you open the file, which is just as well because they all involve subtotals for pitchers which are not intended to be seen anyway.

Now let's begin to breathe life into the beast. Back out to the Design file menu, and choose C for Customize a file. On the Customize a file menu, choose P for Program the form. When you are presented with a facsimile of your form layout, type the following codes in the appropriate fields:

```
relief pitcher: #4
1B: #10
2B: #20
3B: #30
HR: #40
RBI: #50
RUNS: #60
SB: #70
E: #80
HITS: #90=#10+#20+#30+#40
AB: #100
Tot. Hits: #110=@SUM(#90)
Tot. AB: #120=@SUM(#100)
Tot.Bases: #140=#10+(#20*2)+(#30*3)
  +(#40*4)
Tot.Bat.Pts.: #150=(#140+#50+#60+
  #70)-#80
```

APPENDIX

```
   Inn. Pit.: #160
   Earn. Runs: #170
   Comp. Game: #180
   ShO: #190
   WIN: #200
   LOSS: #210
   SAVE: #220
   HITS: #230
   WALKS: #240
   HBP: #250
   Inn.Pts.:#260=#251+#252+#253+#254+
     #255+#256+#257+#258+#259
   Earn. Run Pts.: #270=#261+#262+#263
     +#264+#265+#266+#267+#268+#269
   Bonus Pts.:#290=if#280>0and#280<.51
                     then #290=3;
                   if#280>.5and#280
                   <1.01then #290=2;
                   if#280>1and#280
                   <1.51then#290=1;
                   if#280>1.5and#280
                   <2.01then#290=0;
                   if#280>2and#280
                   <2.51then#290=-1;
                   if#280>2.5and#280
                   <3.01then#290=-2;
                   if#280>3then#290=-3
  Tot. Pit. Pts.: #300=(#180*2)+(#190
                   *2)+(#200*2)+
                   (#220*2)+
                   (#260+#270+
                   #290)-(#210*2)
WHACKO POINTS: #310=#150+#300
```

Once you've caught your breath, you can finish the subtotal calculation fields as follows. Please note that these are set up for seven-inning softball games. If you want to use this template for nine-inning baseball games, you will have to modify the last of each of the following in.sub equations so that they read #251 = -5 . . . #252 = -4 . . . #253 = -3 . . . #254 = -2 . . . #255 = -1 . . . #256 = 0 . . . #257 = 1 . . . #258 = 2 . . . #259 = 3.

```
in.sub1:   #251:if#4=0and#160=1then
   #251=-3
in.sub2: #252:if#4=0and#160=2then
   #252=-2
in.sub3: #253:if#4=0and#160=3then
   #253=-1
in.sub4: #254:if#4=0and#160=4then
   #254=0
in.sub5: #255:if#4=0and#160=5then
   #255=1
in.sub6: #256:if#4=0and#160=6then
   #256=2
in.sub7: #257:if#4=0and#160=7then
   #257=3
in.sub8: #258:if#4=0and#160=8then
   #258=4
in.sub9: #259:if#4=0and#160=9then
   #259=5
```

Courage, man, there's just one more batch of these to go.

```
er.sub1:   #261=if#4=0and#160>0and
   #170=0then#261=6
```

```
er.sub2:    #262=if#4=0and#160>0and
#170>0and#170<5then#262=4
er.sub3:    #263=if#4=0and#160>0and
#170>4and#170<9then#263=3
er.sub4:    #264=if#4=0and#160>0and
#170>9and#170<15then#264=1
er.sub5:    #265=if#4=0and#160>0and
#170>14and#170<20then#265=-1
er.sub6:    #266=if#4=0and#160>0and
#170>19and#170<25then#266=-3
er.sub7:    #267=if#4=0and#160>0and
#170>24and#170<30then#267=-5
er.sub8:    #268=if#4=0and#160>0and
#170>29and#170<35then#267=-6
er.sub9:    #269=if#4=0and#160>0and
#170>34then#267=-8
bo.sub1: #280=(#230+#240+#250)/#160
```

The last set of subtotal calculation fields will also have to be modified if you want to use this file for scoring baseball games, where a respectable ERA is closer to 3 than 30. Below is the series needed for baseball or Rotisserie records.

```
er.sub1:    #261=if#4=0and#160>0and
#170=0then#261=3
er.sub2:    #262=if#4=0and#160>0and
#170=1then#262=2
er.sub3:    #263=if#4=0and#160>0and
#170=2then#263=1
er.sub4:    #264=if#4=0and#160>0and
#170=3then#264=0
er.sub5:    #265=if#4=0and#160>0and
#170=4then#265=-1
```

```
er.sub6:    #266=if#4=0and#160>0and
  #170=5then#266=-2
er.sub7:    #267=if#4=0and#160>0and
  #170=6then#267=-3
er.sub8:    #268=if#4=0and#160>0and
  #170=7then#267=-4
er.sub9:    #269=if#4=0and#160>0and
  #170=8then#267=-5
```

What you've just done is to string the bow of your scoring system. You've created the form into which you'll score your games, with either one record per player per game, or one record per player per at-bat, depending on how whacko you are.

Now return to the main Q&A menu. We're going to create some reports you can use to find out how your players are doing. The first is a report showing cumulative batting records. Choose R for Report and the main Q&A menu. At the main Report menu, choose D for Design/redesign report. If you are not prompted, type the file name or hit return to get a menu of available files.

When the report menu screen comes up, type "batting totals" and hit return. When the Retrieve spec screen comes up, hit F10 to proceed to the Format spec screen. Now you want to type the following codes in the appropriate fields:

```
NAME:1,AS,ST,F(TR,U)
HR: 2,ST,T,F(N1),H(5:HR)
RBI:3,ST,T,F(N1),H(5:RBI)
RUNS:4,ST,T,SA,A,F(N1),H(6:RUNS)
HITS:5,ST,T,SA,A,F(N1),H(6:HITS)
```

```
AB:6,ST,T,SA,A,F(N1),H(7:AB),SC
TOTAL  BATTING  POINTS:7,ST,T,SA,A,F
(N1),H(8:Tot.!Whacko!Pts.)
```

Now hit F8 to access the Derived column screen. Here you want to type the following:

```
Heading: subtotal hits
Formula: @TOTAL(#5,#1)
Column Spec: 8,I
Heading: subtotal abs
Formula: @TOTAL(#6,#1)
Column Spec: 9,I
Heading: BAT.!AVE.
Formula: #8/#9
Column Spec: 10,SA,F(N3)
```

Hit F10 to go to the Print option screen. Change print totals only to "yes." Now hit F8 to get to the Page definition screen. Here you can give your report a header. In the top line of the blank header form, type:

```
@DATE(1)! YOUR TEAM'S NAME Batting Stats
!Page #
```

Hit F10 again, and when you're asked if you want to print your report now, answer no. We need to wait just a little longer before we can do that.

Now, the last thing is to design a report for pitcher performance. Go back to the main Report menu, and choose Design/redesign a report. Call the report Pitcher Totals, and enter "pitcher" (without the quotation marks) in the position field on the Retrieve spec screen.

Hit F10 to go to the Sort spec screen, and enter the following:

```
NAME:1,AS,F(U,TR),H(8:NAME)
Tot.Bat.Pts.:4,ST,H(3:Tot!Bat!Pts),
  F(N0)
Inn.Pit.:4,SA,A,ST,T,F(N1),H(5:Inn
  !Pit),SC
WINS:6,ST,T,F(N0),H(3:Wn)
LOSS:7,ST,F(N0),H(3:Ls)
SAVE:8,ST,T,F(N0),H(3:Sv)
Inn.Pts.:9,ST,SA,F(N1),H(5:Inn!Pts)
Earn.Run Pts.:10,ST,T,SA,F(N1),H(5
  :Earn!Run!Pts)
Bonus Pts.:11,ST,T,SA,F(N1),H(5:
  Bonus!Pts)
Tot.Pitch.Pts.:12,ST,T,SA,F(N1),H
  (6:Tot!Pit!Pts)
WHACKO POINTS:13,ST,T,A,SA,F(N1),H
  (7:Tot!Whacko!Pts)
```

Hit F10 again to proceed to the Report print options screen. Answer yes to the query, Print totals only, along with whatever changes may be necessary for your printer. Hit F8 to go to the Define page screen. In the blank header form, type:

```
@DATE(1)! YOUR TEAM'S NAME Pitching
  Stats !page #
```

Hit F10 again, and then save the report without printing it. So there! Now you've got a database and two report forms for examining your team's performance.

To find out how your starting outfielders are doing, for instance, go to the main Report screen, and hit P for Print a report. Answer yes to the prompt about making temporary changes in the report. Then when the Retrieve spec screen comes up, type the outfielders' names—separated by semicolons—in the name field, and hit F10 until it prints (making whatever other changes you may want to make along the way).

When the dust clears, you'll find that the totals of each player in each major offensive category will be neatly laid out. Depending on your scorekeeping and the capabilities of your printer, you can add more information as you like. The more you play around with the Retrieve spec screen, the more you will find out what your stats have to say.

Want to know if that weak hitting but effective pitcher is a better bet than the one who hits homers but sometimes doesn't have the control to hit the broad side of the backstop? Compare their total Whacko Point scores. There you'll have your answer in simple numerical form.

And as always, the rule is: "The more Whacko, the better."